FISHING FOR PIKE
AND PREDATORS

D L PEGG

To all the 'hardcore' pike and predator
'specialists' out there - I salute you.

CONTENTS

THE STUFF THAT DREAMS ARE MADE OF...

I was fishing a large river just downstream of an impressive waterfall/weirpool... The water was dark coloured and fast flowing... I had never fished here before and didn't quite know what to expect. I had been spinning this spot for about an hour and all to no avail. I took off my 10 gram spinner and replaced it with the biggest, brightest, most over the top obvious lure in my bag... A bright orange and yellow 12 inch 'Bulldawg.' Desperate times call for desperate measures... "Here goes nothing" I thought to myself... I cast out a long way down river and slowly began to retrieve the big lure amongst the deep green of the heavy weed growth. I had taken the large treble hook off of the bottom to "get right in the mix" and prevent getting snagged up on the weeds... I was relying purely on a large single hook built into the main body of the lure... The water was deep and fast flowing with a strong current. After only a few casts... All of a sudden, right out of nowhere a huge pike appeared right in front of me! It came up from the depths, appearing all at once 'hovering menacingly' right behind my bright orange lure! Suddenly, without warning it engulfed my 'bulldawg' in its huge, cavernous mouth!!! In a fraction of a second, my lure disappeared in one explosive, decisive mouthful. For a split second, time stood still... Completely out of character - I turned to my fishing buddy who was standing right next to me (landing net in hand) and shouted loudly at the top of my voice (over the sound of the rushing waterfall) "DID YOU SEE THAT?" "I saw it!" he said with a serious, 'shocked' expression on his face. It was the most striking, incredibly impressive, F-A-S-T pike take that I had ever witnessed in real life in about 25 years of pike fishing. I struck hard, I love this **** I thought to myself. I live for moments like these... This is what I love about pike fishing - the adrenalin - the rush. You can go from 0 to 100 miles per hour in a split second!! In that instant, my fishing rod felt like it had 10,000 volts coursing through it... I was connected to a real 'live wire' the biggest, longest, most impressive, and quite frankly 'massive' pike that I had ever hooked on a lure... And boy oh boy - was she not happy!!!

A REAL 'PREHISTORIC' LAKE MONSTER...

ABOUT THE AUTHOR

My name is Daniel Pegg. I am a 'predator specialist' and all around coarse fisherman. I have been fishing for over thirty years.

For years... I have been making my own fishing tackle and catching fish on home-made spinners, spoons, surface poppers, and hybrid lures...

For the last twenty five years I have specialised in catching predators. My favourite species of fish is the pike (for obvious reasons) closely followed by the perch, trout, chub and catfish. I started out as a young lad fishing for stickleback's with a hand line. I then progressed from catching stickleback's to 'bullyhead's' as we used to call them. From bullhead's to brown and common trout. From trout to roach, perch and barbel. From barbel to bream and carp and from carp to pike, chub, and catfish.

As you can see, I have fished my way from the bottom of the foodchain to the top and caught a broad spectrum of species along the way. I have caught huge grass carp in the Midland's. I have caught ruffe, eel and pike on the Norfolk Broads. I have fished for wild salmon and sea trout on the english coast. I have caught common, brown and rainbow trout "by the bucket load" spinning on the beautiful and majestic river Derwent. I have caught a native brown trout to about five pounds or more and a rainbow trout so big and fat that it spoilt me for life! (Both on home made spinners.) I have fished the river Trent at

Nottingham and caught pike and perch spinning my way (for miles) up and down the Trent canal. I have caught 'specimen' perch, chub and trout on lures.

On one occasion, I had a nice perch take my spinner only for a greedy, opportunist pike to come along and grab it on the way to the bank! Did you ever try landing a pike that wasn't even hooked? It's a rare art form! I once caught a pike that jumped three or four feet straight up into the air and took my lure in mid-air as I was about to cast out again! I have caught a huge catfish in one of many beautiful midlands lake's that was about five feet long and over forty pounds in weight.

I have caught in a landing net (and raised in an aquarium environment) several tiny, minature, newborn 'micro' pike that were so small that at first they had to be fed on tiny, microscopic blood worms! I have kept pike, perch (and coarse fish) on and off for about 14 years. One summer I caught (and raised) four such tiny pike...

Over the last 14 years I have also kept roach, perch, chub, tench, gudgeon, bullhead's, sticklebacks and just about every 'native' species of fish in tanks as pets. I do this for observational/ educational purposes and because (from my youngest days) rivers and lakes have always lay close to my heart and freshwater fish have always held a unique and special fascination for me...

I have caught in a fine mesh hand-net - fish so tiny and young that their bodies were still translucent (see through) and you could not yet tell to which species of fish they actually belonged.

One time I was lucky enough to witness from the bank of a small river, a tiny 'microscopic' shoal of newly hatched silver fish (presumably roach, chub, rudd and dace) being molested by half a dozen or so tiny, newly hatched baby pike!

These fish were so small that you could just (and I do mean just) make out what species they were. At a guess I would say that they measured no more than a centimetre each. I am afraid to say that the newly born pike - attack, harass, molest and predate upon microscopic shoals of tiny silver fish seemingly right from the beginning of their lives, almost from the day that they can first swim. It is just their nature to predate on other fish, it is built into them. I stood on the river bank straining my eyes in amazement and disbelief as I witnessed these tiny pike launch themselves like missiles at will into shoals of dozens of tiny silver fish. The tiny shoal scattered instantly in response only to reform again within seconds! I feel blessed and privileged to have seen what I can only imagine that few people have ever witnessed: New born, tiny pike first learning to hunt and strike at their prey. I stood transfixed for a few minutes until the little shoal moved on... I never saw one of the tiny pike successfully grab or catch a fish inspite of a 'strike' being attempted - almost every few seconds! What an amazing thing for an enthusiastic pike angler to see on a bright, sunny, summer afternoon!

To my knowledge the only freshwater fish that I haven't kept are barbel, carp and eel (an endangered species) ruffe and minnows (we don't get ruffe or minnows where I live) and two non-native species - the wels catfish and the zander. I'm like the Gerald Durrell of the fishing world. Sometimes, I take fish home with me and study them...

Have you ever seen a slow, (sluggish) bottom dwelling, (bottom of the food chain) adult bullhead (millers thumb) successfully grab and try to predate upon a small baby trout? Well I have. After a brief but desperate struggle - the trout managed to escape from the bullhead's mouth. I bet you didn't think it worked that way around did you? Well, neither did I! But you would be surprised - it's dog eat dog in the fish world! Who would have believed it? The bullhead is actually an aggressive little ambush predator! We shouldn't be surprised really - they are a member of the catfish family! The bullhead lies patiently on the riverbed among the pebbles and stones and relies on his excellent 'mottled' camouflage to blend in. To the untrained eye they are almost imperceptible.

You would be amazed at what I have seen...

One of the weirdest things that I have ever seen was while fishing a Scottish Loch in the Highlands... I caught a pike on a homemade spinner... Upon unhooking the pike, I looked down his throat and saw another fish's tail. I pulled out the fish to have a look at what the first pike had been eating... It was another pike! And in that Pike's mouth was another (semi digested) pike! The pike I caught must have grabbed the second pike whilst it was attempting to swallow another pike head first! Talk about opportunistic feeding! That's three pike! Three for the price of one...

Have you ever seen a small shoal of stickleback's harass a young, juvenile pike? I have. They take it in turns to bite the pike's tail fin in order to drive him out of their swim...

One time I was pike fishing and I got talking in depth to a guy who worked for the local environment agency... "You really know your stuff" he said to me. "I had to go to university and get a degree to know some of the stuff you know" he informed me. "I know," I said "but for me there has never been a day of theory, it has all been practical right from the beginning."

Let me start off by saying that there is no 'pseudo-science' here. Everything is based on my own personal research, first hand experience and many, many hours of keen observation... To put it simply... I had to get my own hands dirty...

I have spent many joyous hours of my childhood playing in streams. I have seen quite a few kingfishers over the years, and even a couple of European minks.

I grew up 'tickling' wild brown trout in streams (many years ago) as a youngster. I have caught bullheads, crayfish and stone loach with my hands. I have caught freshwater lamprey's in a hand net. I have even caught freshwater barbel among the silt and tree roots with my bare hands...

As a course fisherman: I have tempted many 'big' carp with float fished bread and worms, cat biscuits, boilies and who knows what? I once even fooled a fifteen pound mirror carp into taking my red and white 'modified' pike plug!

A very happy angler, with a fifteen pound Mirror Carp...

A 'big' Chub 'dwarfs' my size 11 Wellington boot...

I have caught many pike, perch, chub and trout on spinners...
(Often homemade.) I have caught pike and perch on home
made surface poppers (topwater lures.) I have followed the

'humble' (and beloved) river Leen from its source (a natural spring) originating at Newstead Abbey all the way to the Trent with my waders on, carrying a backpack and fishing rod in hand. I have fished amongst the bull rushes and lily pads of beautiful lakes and picturesque ponds deep in the heart of the english countryside... I have spun loch Awe in Scotland. I have float fished, free lined, live baited, dead baited and spun my way from river to pond to lake to sea but most of all I have spun...

I consider 'spinning' or lure fishing for predatory fish to be the most fun, challenging and exciting way to catch fish (especially using topwater or surface lures.) There's just something wild and mysterious about pike and predatory fish and daring to enter into their world to try to outwit them. I love the excitement, the suspense, and the adrenalin rush of a big fish nailing your lure and behaving exactly the way he would do if it was a 'natural' fish in the wild.

I have spent many long sunday afternoon's tinkering with my fishing tackle at the kitchen table! I have accumulated so many fishing lures over the years that I could have filled a skip or started my own lure fishing business! Instead, I have ended up, giving away many lures and bags of fishing tackle to youngsters just starting out... I don't really need them nowadays as I am more than capable of making them myself.

With literally hundreds of captures under my belt, I am a fisherman who has been totally and utterly relentless, willing to walk for miles and fish for hours, with no food, no drink, and no rest. Willing to brave the elements. Not put off by wind, rain, sleet or snow.

Willing to suffer for his art, to experience hunger, thirst, tiredness, dehydration and exhaustion and always willing to make one last cast, come rain or shine, in my never ending quest to catch that 'special' fish.

Me, fishing the Derwent in the summer of 2013...

When I was younger I used to fast while I fished - no food and no drink. It was not a religious or spiritual discipline. It was just that I got so focussed on what I was doing, so single minded, so completely engrossed - obsessed even, that I did not have time to stop, rest, eat or drink. I could do that when I got home! Fishing has always had that effect on me. Time stands still and nothing else matters. There simply aren't enough hours in the day. I am the kind of man who can happily fish from dawn till dusk... (And beyond...) If the right opportunity presents itself!

Many times when I have been out fishing with my friend, he has said to me "right then, time to pack up and head home" to which I would reply "is it that time already?" "We have been fishing non-stop for hours!" he would say. "yeah, but it only seemed like five minutes though didn't it?" I would reply.

For me, going fishing is like being in love... A man who is in love does not feel the need for food or drink or rest. All he needs is to be in the presence of his beloved - to make him feel alive again! And after all these years, I am still in love with my fishing! It still makes me feel alive, it is still my passion.

I fish the way I live - with deep passion and unrelenting energy...
I believe that I have paid my dues as an angler over the past
thirty years or so and earned the right to write this book and tell
my stories.

I hope you enjoy reading my book and listening to my stories,
and most of all, I hope they inspire you to go out fishing again...

Enjoy!

The Author.

INTRODUCTION

I saw my first pike when I was a young lad...

I remember it now - like it was yesterday, even though it is over 30 years ago...

I'll never forget... When we were kids, me and my friends used to go to Newstead Abbey at the weekends...

One day I was looking into the water by some overgrown bushes and I saw this mean looking creature with green and yellow camouflage on its back. It was long and pencil thin, just laying there motionless right beneath the surface of the water... I said to my friend who was about three years older than me, "come quick and see this, I've found a snake." He came and looked at the green and yellow creature with camouflage on it's back. "That's not a snake" he said, "it's a pike." It sounds funny now, but anyone who has ever seen a pike up close with it's long, streamlined body, large eyes and duck like bill, plus beautifully marked green and yellow camouflage patterns, could understand how a young boy could upon first sight of the pike have mistaken him for a snake!

And thus began a lifelong fascination and obsession with pike, and pike fishing that has led me to the capture of countless pike along the way, along with specimen perch, trout, chub and catfish! And even a photographed fifteen pound mirror carp, taken on a modified red and white pike plug, hooked in the mouth, as seen and verified by six witnesses who were present at the time of capture!

Whilst the majority of these predators have been caught on lures - many of them home-made. The author has also become proficient at stalking fish and catching them with both live and dead baits. Having also spent considerable time observing both pike, perch (and most other native species) in an aquarium environment for the last fourteen years, feels more than qualified to speak about these matters in great detail... Being an all around angler with over thirty years fishing experience, as well as a predator 'specialist' and specimen hunter. A relentless pike fisherman, and a man who has spent his lifetime studying and observing pike and pike behaviour and also the various means by which they may be caught. What could be more interesting than studying and catching these 'magnificent' creatures?

CHAPTER 1.
EARLY DAYS

<u>NEWSTEAD ABBEY</u>

After that day, me and my friends returned to Newstead Abbey many times...

We used to sit and observe the fish all day long on Saturdays and Sundays. Two or three of us used to hang over the bridge, that the stream ran underneath, near the big lake and watch the fish. We used to fish for them with hand lines. I can still remember, we used little tiny size 16 hooks and little blue spools of Bayer Perlon line bought from Tony Greaves tackle shop in Hucknall, Nottingham, which is no longer there now, but as I remember it used to have a picture of a pike 'tail walking' above the window. We used mixed maggots for bait which used to get molested by the little sticklebacks and minnows. Now and then we would hook a little half a pound roach which we would pull up flapping about all over the place. More often than not these little fish would slip off the hook before we could get our grubby little hands on them! It is difficult to describe the excitement we all felt, and the joy that visits to Newstead Abbey would bring to our hearts. I can still remember that same feeling of excitement that I used to get when I see a little, blue, Bayer Perlon, spool of line and remember those little roach flapping about all over the place!

Little by little, we began to notice what an intense interest those mean looking, dark green, pike had in our little roach.

We noticed how patient they were, and how they could lay still and motionless for hours, seemingly for an eternity, just lazing about doing nothing, as if they were dead, or paralyzed, or completely incapable of movement. Later we learned that this is just a ploy that the pike uses. He lays perfectly still for hours, days even. When he does move he just drifts slowly, subtly and lazily at first, as if he has no real purpose or motive. He does however, have a purpose, and that purpose is to creep up closer on the unsuspecting shoals of prey fish, or to place himself into a better position from which to project himself like a missile and ambush his prey. All of this is to lull the shoals of docile prey fish into a false sense of security. Little by little the prey fish would forget previous encounters and begin to drift closer and closer into the danger zone, and towards the pike. Then when the moment is just right, and they have completely let their guard down, he plays his hand, and launches himself at full speed, like a torpedo, with his mouth gaping wide open to catch his unsuspecting prey.

Top Tip: If you are spinning and you see a cloud of small bubbles rising just behind your lure - then the chances are that a pike has just attacked (and missed) your lure! Fear not, all is not lost - just cast your lure back into the swim - right behind the cloud of bubbles and reel slowly, oh and hold on tight!

YOUNG SCALLIES

Me and my friends worked on a local farm when I was fourteen years old. I used to finish school at a quarter to four and be on the farm by five o clock and work till eight pm, potato picking and shoveling soil five days a week. It was back breaking work... That farmer certainly got his moneys worth out of us! The way I saw it, he owed us big time...

We took advantage of free fishing whenever we could but affording to join a local club was out of the question. If you had accused me of poaching I wouldn't have known what you were talking about. We just fished wherever we could. Wherever there was water and potentially fish. We never noticed any signs and even when we did we never paid any mind. After all, how is a young kid supposed to know what big words like private, syndicate, prosecute and summons mean? I still remember those words though don't I? I suppose it's because I never really understood them, they were such a mystery to me, they must have left me curious and intrigued!

I suppose I was a bit of a young scally back in those days but as time went on I preferred to think of myself as less of a scoundrel and more of a loveable rogue! Me and the local farmers had an unspoken agreement... They didn't bother me, as long as they didn't catch me fishing their ponds!! The thing is - a farmer can't be everywhere all at once - he is not omnipresent! He is a very busy man but there is just not enough of him to go around... So I figured what he doesn't know - won't hurt him and I fished his waters on a sort of "catch me if you can" basis. Only, what I didn't count on, was that farmers are crafty old buggers, and they carry guns, and they take fishing on their land very seriously indeed - a lot more seriously than I was taking it! As you will soon see...

RIDING SHOTGUN...

I never really considered myself a poacher. I considered myself a sport fisherman. I fished for fun, for amusement, entertainment, recreation and leisure. It's a shame the local farmer didn't see it that way...

I was fishing a deep pond on the edge of a farmer's field. What I thought was an irrigation pond used by the farmer for watering his crops... I baited my hook with a big, fat juicy worm and sat silently watching my float. I thought to myself: "If the farmer comes I'll hear the engine on his land rover." Unfortunately for me, that wily, old farmer was a lot shrewder than I was. He turned off his engine and rolled silently down the hill to the spot where I was fishing and caught me red handed!

The first time he caught me he gave me a strict reprimand: "Do you think these fish got in here all by themselves?" He said, and saw me on my merry way.

The second time he caught me one dark evening, on my way home, following the river through one of his fields. He put his lights on full beam and pulled up right in front of me in his land rover. He had a double barrelled shotgun strapped around his shoulder and two great big dogs! He was not happy! "What do you think you're doing?" he asked "This is private land and you're trespassing." Farmers! They all say the same thing, don't they? I just shrugged, "just taking a short cut home" was all I could manage to say. "Well, don't let me catch you round here again" he said, "I won't" I said and I meant it.

The third time he caught me... I know, I know, some people never learn do they? But you can't put an old head on young shoulders can you? That sneaky old farmer was wiser than me, wasn't he? And the cards were stacked against me... The only thing I had going for me was youth, daring and downright audacity... That and my foolish persistance!

In my defence: It was a long, long, time ago and I was 'lured to his pond' by the promise of huge, big, fat, greedy, four or five pound plus, cannibalistic, specimen perch!

Where else can you go to catch a perch like that? One day (almost twenty five years ago now) I was float fishing his pond with a big, fat, juicy, lobworm, as usual...

I had the hot sun on my back and I was staring at my float and sort of daydreaming about what might be down there... Big perch were the order of the day and I was feeling lucky punk. Unfortunately for me - it was not to be, my luck was about to run out! I saw a big flash - like when someone shines the reflection of the sun in your eyes with a watch or a mirror... I casually looked up from my float to the other side of the pond. It was my old

friend the farmer... He had sneaked up on me (again!) with his engine turned off. This time, he was looking at me through the sight's of his shotgun! It was the reflection of the sun behind me shining on the glass of his telescopic rifle sight that had flashed in my eyes! I started to reel in my float, as fast as I could... "He wouldn't" I thought to myself. "He couldn't" I thought to myself... Pow! He could! I grabbed my bag, and ran for the bushes as fast as I could, with a long trail of line left dangling behind me. He fired three or four more 'warning' shots at me in quick succession... You see, I think that the farmer, had been trying, to give me a 'subtle' message. Only, I wasn't quite getting the message! Perhaps my neurons weren't firing properly or something. "No fishing!" Big perch! "NO FISHING!" But - BIG PERCH!!
<u>"NO FISHING!"</u>

BUT WHAT ABOUT ALL THE BIG PERCH!!!

I got the message this time. The farmer was playing hardball, he "insisted" I leave, and he wasn't taking no for an answer. I ran through the trees and up the steep bank of the hill with the sounds of gun shots, in the distance behind me, still ringing in my ears. I do not know whether he was shooting to hit or just shooting to scare me but I did know one thing for sure - I wasn't hanging around to find out! I don't hold it against him - even though he saw fit to use me for target practise! Joking aside, with hindsight, if he wanted to hit me, he could have hit me at will. Farmers shoot pheasants, partridges and wood pigeons as well as other things all of the time. I bet he got a good laugh out of me that day, scrambling up that steep bank, with my tail between my legs. I bet he thought to himself "I bet that's the last I'll see of that young scally, he he he." Little did he know... What is it they say? If at first you don't succeed... Try, try again!

As a side note: I have nothing against farmers. I used to work on a farm. In fact, an old mate of mine is the son of a farmer - it's a funny old world i'nt it!

A HUGE PERCH AND A BENT HOOK...

One sunny day, me and my brothers met up with a couple of other lads who worked alongside my brother at the local fishing tackle shop and went out fishing together. We were fishing this deep, 'interesting' (farmers) pond that was full of shoals of big carp as well as some very big specimen perch and trout! Some days the water was crystal clear, and other days the colour of clay. There had been some heavy rain recently, so the water was brown and heavily coloured on the day that we were fishing. This pond had seen a recent explosion of small perch. This does tend to happen every so often in certain places every so many years. This leads to big perch, predating on the smaller perch. Which in turn results in some captures of some very big perch. We caught plenty of small perch and half a pounder's. Every so often we would hit something bigger. When the water was crystal clear you could see the bigger perch regurgitating their smaller brethren on their way to the bank. Every decent perch we caught had a perch tail hanging out of the back of it's throat. On this particular day we had all decided to float fish worms on account of the recent, heavy rainfall. The majority of our fishing consisted of whipping out small, greedy perch from the side of the bank. With the odd pounder and carp thrown in for good measure. If I knew then what I know now! I would have put on the first small perch that I caught, and used it for bait, but this is going back twenty five years now...

My brother who is a very careful and patient fisherman was sat watching his float. When all of a sudden, it went under. He struck at once, but instead of swinging out a little perch as we had become accustomed to by now, his float stayed underwater and refused to come back up to the surface. "I'm in!" he said and began to carefully, patiently play what he thought was a carp. Full credit to him, he never 'bullies' his fish in and always takes his time to play them in properly, being careful not to lose them.

After five or ten minutes or so, everyone had put their rods down and gathered around to see what he had hooked. He was trying to pull the fish up to the surface so that we could all have a look at what he had hooked but the fish was having none of it. Every time he raised his rod and put some pressure on the fish it just pulled back and digged down deeper, towards the bottom. Now this was a very deep pond with steep banks. When my brother did eventually manage to bring this fish up to the surface we were all in for a big shock...

Instead of the 10 pound odd carp that we were all expecting to see, was the biggest perch that you have ever seen in your life, and when I say 'big' I mean BIG - abnormally big! It was thick and wide, and fat and round - like an over-inflated rugby ball. It was hump backed and pot bellied with five or six unmistakable big black bars across the side of its body. It had big yellow eyes and a mouth the size of a bucket...

None of us had ever seen anything like it before and if I am completely honest I have never seen anything quite like it (in real life) ever since. Now, I have caught lots of big perch whilst spinning for pike on plugs and surface poppers, spinners and even pike spoons, but like I said, this fish was different, this fish was special, this was the perch of a lifetime - the stuff that dreams are made of.

Upon seeing the fish, we all began screaming at my brother in excitement and all talking at the same time, telling him "do not lose this fish, do not lose this fish, don't you dare lose this fish, you will never hook another fish like this in your life, this could be a new british record" and so on and so forth. I am not exaggerating. I really believe that perch could have been the british record. I have got no reason to lie. I am not the one that hooked it. We may all have been a lot younger then but we all knew that this was no ordinary fish.

My brother lost it. We couldn't believe it. We were all blaming him for losing the fish until we examined his hook.

That perch had bent his hook straight!!! I told you it was a big fish!

I recently spoke to a man, who worked at our local tackle shop for some years... He is a fisherman of some renown, well known and well respected. He has caught some very, very big fish. He worked alongside my brother for several years. He was there that day when my brother hooked the biggest perch that any of us has ever seen... I asked him to give me a realistic, conservative estimate of how big he thinks that huge perch was. He said that he was 'certain' that it would have weighed no less than five and a half pounds! Now bear in mind that this was about 25 years ago in the year 1999 or 2000. I don't know what the exact british record perch was back then but the last time I checked, it was about six pounds and two or three ounces. You do the maths... It would have been close, very close and if my brother had, had a better quality hook on we might have broke the british record!! He never was the sharpest tool in the box! But then again: I could kick myself for some of the fish I've lost!!

RAZOR BACK - THE ONE THAT DIDN'T GET AWAY!

A monster deep water perch caught on a fluttering blue pike spoon...

After this, my friend's grandad (a man from another time) heard about my brother's experience with the huge perch and specifically asked my friend to catch him a big perch for the dinner table! Don't ask... Not my first choice, but apparently people used to eat them, back in the day...

My friend (who also worked in the fishing tackle shop) was only about sixteen years old at the time wanted to put a big smile on his old grandad's face and so we set off to catch a big perch for his grandad's supper! Me and my friend decided to (throw caution to the wind as usual) and spin the same deep pond on a sunny summers day. My friend decided use a big, blue pike spoon. He began casting out towards the central island, and reeling in, in a haphazard, unpredictable way. Nothing much was happening, when all of a sudden - he was in! A big, broad perch with a mouth the size of a bucket had took his shiny blue pike spoon...

As he began to pull in this big perch, we noticed something strange and out of the ordinary... The big perch was regurgitating small perch (three - four inches long perch) out of his mouth all the way in! I have never seen anything like this phenomenon before or since except on this pond, where there had been a recent 'explosion' of small perch everywhere. I have witnessed both specimen perch and trout display exactly the same behaviour on this deep pond but never anywhere else. Although I have read about this phenomena occuring historically every so many years when perch breed and there is an explosion in perch numbers, you have the perfect environment to catch some very big perch and other predators inhabiting the same water due to the presence of so much readily available 'food' in the form of small, young, immature perch. My friend landed the big perch which was full of little perch! It even had a perch's tail hanging out of the back of its throat!

Again, on this water any sizable perch or trout caught may regurgitate perch on the way in and would always - beyond doubt have a perch's tail hanging out of the back of it's throat! My friend then took the perch home for his grandad. Now, I have to say that the above mentioned perch is THE biggest perch that I have ever seen (landed) in real life, in over thirty years of fishing. I looked at my watch, it had taken exactly twenty minutes to catch this fish. My friend's grandad informed us that when he gutted that big, old perch for the dinner table, he found another four or five half digested perch in it's belly! No surprises there.

I bet my friend's old grandad couldn't believe his eyes when he saw that perch. I bet he had never seen a perch like it in his entire life. He must have had a feast! Catching a huge perch in a place like that does not require a great amount of skill. In fact, anybody could do it, where it not for the fact that not that many places exist with this unique environment and it's perfect properties/qualities that produce such truly specimen perch.

Not many people are blessed enough or fortunate enough to fish water's like this in their lifetime. And nor would we have been if not for our 'brass balls.' We were lucky, but I bet it isn't the same place anymore. Now, like I say, this unusual phenomenon only occurs once every so many years or even decades in a few unique places. And that is why we were willing to look down the barrell of a shotgun and risk being shot at by angry farmer's... We were close to breaking the british perch record (and we knew it) and I can confidently say "we came within a hairs breadth of breaking it!" (If only I knew then what I know now!) But then again, it wasn't the smartest decision I have ever made! I probably wouldn't have the minerals to face down an angry farmer these days!

BIG BROWNIES

When we first fished this water I was after pike, not knowing that there are no pike in this pond, which is one of the reasons why the perch (and trout) grew so big. I had on a small (four inch) brown trout imitation, plastic, shallow diving plug. I was casting out towards the central island (about the only feature on the pond) and kept getting takes that seemed to let go every few seconds. When my lure came into sight, I could see in the crystal clear water that a native brown trout of two or three pounds kept pecking at and attempting to take my lure over and over again repeatedly...

We caught a few of these big 'brownies' and again they were displaying the unusual phenomena of regurgititating small perch on the way in. Again, they always had a perch tail hanging out of the back of their throat's and lastly the one or two that we took home for the dinner table always had a belly full of four or five half digested perch! There were also some large carp in that pond - twenty plus pounders and you can well imagine what they were eating can't you...

If I knew then what I know now, I would have used perch livebait, perch deadbait, small perch fished sink and draw fashion or the most lifelike plastic or rubber perch imitation lure that could be found. Oh well, you live and you learn, you can't put an old head on young shoulders can you? As the saying goes: We grow too fast old and too slow smart...

GET AWFF MY LAIND!!!!!

I have two younger brothers, who were quite into fishing when we were growing up. One of them still is. One of my brothers, worked in the local fishing tackle shop for several years. My youngest brother's personal best pike is twenty four pounds. Pretty good you might say but I come from a fishing family and my uncle Philip has caught a thirty eight pound pike! Now I, more than most other people know just what an achievement this is. A thirty eight pounder is truly a once in a lifetime fish!! I don't think any of us will ever top that! He has simply raised the bar too high!

Growing up, my younger brothers used to borrow my fishing tackle without asking! One time, I knew that the young scallies were fishing for carp, in a place, where they ought not to be...

I asked my mum where my fishing tackle was and she informed me that the pair of them had "took the lot" and gone fishing with another lad who worked in the local tackle shop. I asked her where they had gone? "Poachers palace" she informed me. The stuff of legends, a far off place - a carp fisherman's dream come true.

I quickly formulated a crafty plan. "Lets go up there and scare them" I said to my friend. The pair of us sneaked up behind them, and hid behind some bushes, in a farmers field, which overlooked the would be carpers lake. In my best 'farmers voice' I shouted at the top of my lungs "Oi, get awff my laind!!!!! The three of them had it away on their toes and legged it towards their bikes, without so much as a glance backwards to see if it was indeed the farmer. They set a pace that Linford Christie would have been proud of. I ran after them shouting "wait, it's only me, wait, wait come back, it's me, your brother!" but it was all to no avail, It was too late. They had it away, on their bicycles and left me behind in a cloud of dust. There was no sign of them! I stood there alone in a cloud of dust. Not a literal cloud of dust - an ACTUAL **cloud of dust.** I stood their laughing, and choking at the same time. Them three are in the wrong sport, I thought to myself, They ought to have been Ironman tri-athletes.

What's worse is that they had left all their tackle behind - rods, reels, bags, everything. The worst part is, that it wasn't even their tackle - it was mine! I'd certainly think twice about lending them anything in future! and when I went over and checked the rods - one of them had a carp on the end of it! Needless to say, It was my honourable duty to reel that carp in and release it before reeling in all the lines and lugging all the tackle, the long trek back home.

When I got back home, I hid all the tackle, and asked the young rascals what they had been up to? And why they were all back so soon? And if they had caught anything? And where was all my tackle? They informed me that they had got caught poaching. "By who?" I said. "By the farmer" they answered. "But you got away, all right?" I asked. "Yeah, we escaped on our bikes." they said. "And, you brought all my fishing tackle back home with you, safe and sound?" I quizzed. "No" they said. "What do you mean - no?" I asked. "We left it all behind at the pond." You should have seen their faces. I couldn't keep it up any longer, so I blurted out the truth - "It was me, you fools, and a good job it was as well too, or you lot would be replacing all my fishing tackle!"

"You B*****d" they said. "We had only just set up as well, and then we had to peddle our bikes, all the way back home." "That'll teach you young scallies to borrow my fishing tackle, without asking, to go poaching with, then won't it?" I said. "Never mind, I reeled in that big carp for you anyway." "What?" they asked. "I did the business for you with that big carp that you left on the end of your line, when you ran off." "Thanks" they said. "No problem," I said. "What are big brothers for?"

Needless to say, they didn't find it as funny as we did, but I think me mam saw the funny side, and got a good laugh out of it and to be honest I think they were just relieved that they didn't have to replace all my fishing tackle out of their own pockets!

So the moral of the story is this: Always use your own fishing tackle when you go poaching! No, no, that doesn't sound right, does it? The moral of the story is: Make sure you check that it really is the farmer that's caught you poaching and not your brother, or one of your mates playing a practical joke on you and having a good old laugh at your expense!

You know what the moral of the story is - you don't need me to tell you!

<u>RAISED ON PIKE AND STORIES OF IRISH PIKE!</u>

My family was raised on pike and stories of Irish pike...
My grandfather was Irish and my grandmother, mother and her four siblings all lived and grew up in Ireland. Our family name was Mulholland. Back in those days, times were hard and men were men. My grandfather was a pike fisherman and later on a fly fisherman (for trout.) He had a bad leg from having polio as a child. His calf muscle wasted away and never grew back as a result of the polio.

Nowadays they might have said that he was disabled but my grandad never saw himself like that... He was a very proud man and never let his bad leg slow him down, or stop him from doing what he wanted to do. My mum says that someone once made the mistake of calling him a cripple! The man's feet never touched the ground! My Grandfather was 6ft tall and worked hard all his life. He often worked 12 hours a day, 7 days a week. My mother used to say that he did the work of three men all by himself! He used to cycle down to the local river most days after work in the evenings, to go fishing for pike with his eldest son (my uncle Phil.) In those days, people used to eat whatever they caught - especially Irish river pike!

EARTHY PIKE IN SALTWATER BUCKETS!

There's an old story in our family handed down by my grandparents about a big pike left to stew in a bucket of salt water overnight and 5 hungry, inquisitive children (one of whom was my mother...)

My grandmother used to tell it best... It goes something like this...

My grandfather went out fishing one evening after work. He was after pike as usual. He was successful on this occasion and brought home a big Irish river pike for supper. My grandparents always used to say that the pike is a very earthy fish. On account of this, they used to leave it to soak in a bucket of salt water overnight. My mother was one of five children - three girls and two boys. The children all gathered around to see what their father had brought home in his bag. "Ugh, what a big, ugly fish!" one of them said. "I'm not eating that," said another, "it looks disgusting," said a third, "all green and slimy."

GRANDMA'S PIKE FISHCAKES

The next day, all was forgotten. The family sat down together, as usual, to eat their evening meal. Tonight it was fishcakes. "Mum, these are yummy" said one of the children. At the end of the meal the children thanked their mother for her delicious cooking. "Mum, where did you get those delicious fish cakes from?" asked one of the children. "Do you remember that big, ugly, green fish?" replied my grandma, "Yes" they replied. "Well you just ate it!" she said. "Urghh!" said one and all!

A PIKE FOR TEA!

Having heard so many stories about catching pike and eating them (and since it was almost a family tradition!) I decided to try one for myself and see what all the fuss was about. When I was young, I caught a small jack pike of about two pounds or so in a local river and brought it back to my mums house to eat... "What's that you've got?" my mum asked. "A pike" I replied. "What are you going to do with it?" asked my mum. "You're going to cook it for me!" I replied. "Okay" she said. My mum gutted the pike for me and prepared it for my tea! We had a cat called kitty (of all things) at the time. As my mum was preparing the pike, kitty would not leave the kitchen the whole time, and wouldn't stop begging! I was very surprised by this as I had recently brought home a two and a half pound brown trout and kitty wasn't interested in my trout in the slightest and never even batted an eyelid.

When the pike was cooked me and my mum gave kitty a bowl full of pike (to stop her whining) which she proceeded to snaffle in record time and then came back begging for more! We gave her another bowl which she also ate and fast. Amazingly - my cat loved pike! I wasn't quite so impressed! I don't know whether it was the 'earthy' flavour of the pike, or if my mum had overcooked it but that pike tasted like rubber to me! I was not impressed! Needless to say, I cannot recall ever eating another pike since!

THE WELSH FELLA

I used to live next door to this old welsh fella... One day, I was off out the door 'piking' when he stopped me. "Where are you going?" He asked. "I'm off piking... Why? You coming?" I said. "No, I'm not fit enough, he said. "Catch me a pike and I'll have it for me tea!" "Are you serious?" I asked. "Definitely" he said. "Okay then I said, I'll see what I can do..."

I caught a pike of about 5 pounds or so on a small (floating) rubber lizard of all things! I simply put a size six treble in its head and used it as a lure! I arrived back home and gave my neighbour a knock... I showed him the 5 pounder "Is that good enough for you?" I asked. A big smile spread across his face, "that's lovely, that is!" he said. He took it straight indoors and set about preparing it for the dinner table! I started unpacking my fishing tackle and thought no more about it. I saw him either that evening or the next day and he showed me his handiwork... He had cut the pike up into fillets and put it in his fridge and freezer! I asked him what it was like... He told me that he had it with chips for his tea, and that it was lovely! Another satisfied customer! (Rather him than me!)

BIG WORMS AND NOSE DIVING PIKE...

When I first got interested in pike fishing as a youngster, I told my old grandad about our little adventures and how we sometimes struggled to catch bait for pike fishing...

"What can I catch pike on?" I asked him. His answer surprised me. "Worms" he said. "What?" I asked. "You can catch pike on worms?" He said "Worms?" I said." Worms" He replied.

I can't blame him for recommending worms to us... Given the luxury of a few lures we would have probably taken someone's eye out! My grandad was a man of few words but very wise. It wasn't long until I put my grandad's advice to good use...

When I next saw my friends, I told them what my old grandad had said. The next time we visited Newstead Abbey, Instead of spending hours on end trying to catch a roach, or a perch for bait, we just gathered as many big worms as we could find and stuck them on the biggest hook that we could find (a bronzed size 2.) We were still using blue, Bayer Perlon hand lines (none of us owned a real fishing rod.) and still using single hooks (none of us had ever seen or heard of a treble hook.) My grandad was right: pike love worms! The bigger - the better!

Every time we threw out our worm baited hook, a big pike would come over to investigate what the splash was... He would then nose dive, facedown and tail up, and scoop up our 'giant octopus' worm bait hook offering. This happened everytime. The pike was not aggressive and did not attack the worms. He just seemed to recognise them for what they were - a nice, easy, free meal that stood no chance of getting away. He readily accepted them for the welcome protein and energy source that they are. Not a big meal, just a welcome snack. Perhaps, he scooped them up in this way so as not to reveal his true nature and aggressive, predatory instinct to any prey fish that were looking in his direction.

PIKE ON THE FLY (ALMOST) AT NEWSTEAD ABBEY

Another time, me and my friends were fishing Newstead Abbey. We had no bait and I came up with an idea. I wondered around on the grass bank near the water (where some peacocks roamed freely about) and found a peacock feather. I tied the peacock feather to a large, single, (size two) hook to make an attractive but somewhat primitive, makeshift pike fly. I then attached some weights, wet it, and cast it out towards the bushes on the far side of the bank. Imagine my surprise when, I started to pull in my home made pike fly by hand and not one but THREE pike came out from under the bushes to investigate and started following my lure! I never managed to catch a pike on my home-made pike fly that day but not for want of trying! I guess I just didn't have the skill to fool the pike into taking my peacock feather or the right tools for that matter but I whiled away a good hour trying all the same! I like to think that, in some ways, I was on the right track, thinking correctly, and years ahead of my time... After all, I never really had anyone to teach me how to fish properly - none of us did - it was all a learning curve, trial and error, and what I like to call 'natural progression.' My old grandad gave me a few useful tips... But I had to implement them by myself.

THE 'MONSTER'

A few months ago, I caught a small Jack pike, of about 3 or 4lb's, on a shallow diving lure, in a small river. This is nothing unusual for me. It has happened many times. What was different about this encounter, I am about to relay...

As I was landing this little monster a couple came walking along the bank with their young son who must have been around 6 or 7 years old. "Look," said the mother, "that man has caught a fish!" Nothing unusual about that either, happens all the time. What was unusual, was this young lad's reaction...

He was staring - 'gobsmacked' in complete amazement. His mouth was hanging wide open, and he was staring at the pike in a stunned silence. He had a big bottle of pop in his right hand, and he was oblivious to the fact that, he was pointing it downwards, and spilling it all over the ground! I tried to point this out to his parents, who in turn tried to point it out to their son, but he was completely unaware of anything except the pike!

This took me back, to something that happened to me, over thirty years ago...

Me and my friends, were at Newstead Abbey, one Saturday, on our own (no parental supervision in those days.) We hooked a BIG pike on the lower lake, near the gardens, on a big brass coloured size 2 hook and a blue spool of good old Bayer Perlon hand line! We lost the pike! He snapped our hand line! We went home and told all our friends, and guess what? Nobody believed that we had really hooked 'the monster.'

Shortly after that, I inherited an old wooden sea fishing reel and some blue, 30 or so pound breaking strain, sea fishing line from a neighbour...

Back we went, one of us threw out the worm baited hook (which looked like a slimy wriggling octopus.) Out came the pike again. It was 'the big one' - the 'monster.' He came over to investigate our worm cocktail/octopus hook bait offering... Suddenly he 'nose dived' and took the worms! We pulled him in, quickly on the sea fishing line and landed him safely on the bank. We looked him over and sure enough, not one, but two big brass coloured size two hooks - this was the same fish, that we had lost previously. We looked at each other and all knew in an instant what each other was thinking... This was a trophy fish! we had to take it back home, and show people, or nobody would ever believe us! We put him in a back pack and set off on the long walk home...

When we got home we went straight around to our friend's house who was 3 years older than me and regarded by one and all as 'our leader.' He lived about 3 houses up the street from me. His father was a right character, one of those old school, old fashioned, unusual, eccentric types that you hardly ever see or meet any more. He drove a range rover (which was much rarer in those days.) He was always wearing army camouflage clothes, wellies and boots, he wore hats with (fly fishing) flies attached to them. He kept guns and went out shooting with a 12 bore, double barrel shotgun. He always had pheasants, wood pigeons, partridges, rabbits or hares hanging up on a hook outside his back door. His kitchen often smelt of rabbit or hare cooking (not a pleasant smell if you ask me.) He kept owls, hawks and other birds of prey in cages on his back garden. You'd see him with a protective leather glove on and a great big scary looking bird with these huge claws sat perched on a stick with a lead attached to it so it couldn't fly off. He had a freezer in his outhouse full of some of the biggest, fattest trout that you had ever seen in your life! but he would never breathe a whisper to a soul about where he had caught them from. He was a very quiet man and always seemed to talk in riddles around us. He spoke of far off places with far fetched and wonderful sounding names such as 'pike lake' and 'poachers palace.' He even kept ferrets. A right character. He used to go out hunting, and shooting with one of our other neighbours across the street - a grand old man with an old deaf dog (deaf from being taken out on one too many shooting expeditions.) Such were the types of characters that I grew up with at such an impressionable age... I bet they could tell you a story or two.

Back to my story...

We knocked on the door and walked into our friends kitchen. "Come see what we have caught" we said. My friend and his dad walked into the kitchen. "What have you caught?" they asked. "A great big, monster pike" we said "the big one that we told you about, the one from Newstead Abbey!" "Let's have a look then" my friends dad said. My friend pulled the 'monster' out of his back pack and placed it down gently on the kitchen work surface. We stood back, proud as punch and admired our "capture."

All of a sudden, my friend's dad screamed "He's still alive" and proceeded to whack it on the head with his cane! In the process of making sure that the pike was indeed dead. "He's dead now" said my friends dad. "It was probably just his nerves."

"He's not a monster" my friends dad said, "he's only a baby." "He's huge" we protested. "Hang on a minute", my friends dad said " I'll go and get the scales." He weighed the pike carefully, "four pounds" he said as if to settle the argument. It didn't sound like a lot but we didn't care, we knew better. I was there and I remember - that pike was huge, he was a monster. He might have been a "baby" or a "tiddler" to our friends dad, but to us - a bunch of kids - he was the catch of a lifetime, the stuff that dreams are made of... A real life monster...

CATCHING MUSKIES IN CANADA!

Now and again, I bump into one of my old friends that I used to fish Newstead Abbey with as a child. He always stops to speak to me and ask me if I have been fishing lately. Sometimes we talk about the old days. I get carried away sometimes talking about "those big old pike we used to catch up Newstead Abbey." One time, he stopped me mid-sentence... "I know, I was there" he reminded me. He informed me that he had been fishing the same lake that I had been fishing recently... Any good? I asked "I caught a 22lb pike on a miniature Budweiser can imitation surface popper" he replied. "Unbelievable" I said. "Yeah, took me about 50 casts to get a take though" he said. He told me, he has even been fishing in Canada for Muskies!

I think that our childhood experiences with those big pike must have left a long lasting impression on us! After all, we've been fishing for them ever since!

THE DEFORMED PIKE

Another interesting story he told me was about a pike he caught with an unusual, abnormal, 'deformed' appearance. It had a giant head, and a long, lean, withered body! He was lure fishing one day and he caught a pike with a big old head on it and a long, skinny, malnourished body. The pike, which was lightly hooked in the side of the mouth, didn't put up much of a fight and must have been badly out of condition - by all accounts it looked as if it had been starving! The mystery was soon unravelled when he tried to open the pike's mouth to unhook it... It had a big pike plug (somebody else's) stuck in it's mouth, and had been unable to hunt or feed properly due to the obstruction. Somebody had obviously hooked it at one time or another and been snapped off in the ensuing struggle. The big pike was left with a big plug stuck in its jaws and was unable to hunt or feed properly. The big plug was physically blocking the pikes throat so as to make it impossible for the pike to swallow anything it caught! The poor thing was starving and half dead by the time my friend caught it.

It was lucky for the pike that he did catch it in time before it died of starvation! He told me that the fish he caught was obviously once a big fish as he could easily tell by the size of its head and mouth and by the length of it. But it had obviously gone without food for quite some time as evidenced by its 'withered' out of condition appearance. The difference between the size of its head and the size of its body was so striking as to make it look physically deformed. My friend carefully unhooked it and gently released it back into the wild to make a full recovery and a full return to its former glory.

My younger brother, who is also an avid pike fishermen has had a similiar experience... He once caught a pike whilst deadbaiting on the bottom of a lake. He began to unhook it and quickly realised that there were two sets of trebles in the pikes mouth! Again, somebody else had been snapped off in the tussle of a previous encounter with the same fish.

It is easy to judge these occurrences as being the result of incompetence, carelessness, recklessness or foolishness but you never can tell. Sometimes it is carelessness or incompetence, other times it is just sheer bad luck. After all - a pike can be a very strong, heavily muscled fish - a fish that lives on a diet of almost pure protein and rests almost all of the time. Ten, twenty, or even thirty pounds or so of well fed, well rested, lightning fast, torpedo shaped muscle, with nearly all of its large, powerful fins situated at the back of its body - near that powerhouse of a tail for quick fire, rapid bursts of acceleration. A fish that is faster than all other freshwater fish. Indeed, the fastest swimming freshwater fish on earth bar none. A fish that is more than capable of swimming in quick bursts of speed reaching up to 40 kilometres per hour. It is easy to underestimate them - but they are not to be underestimated! If your line or knot is not strong enough, if your drag is not set properly or if you are just plain caught off guard - a breakage is the likely end result!

Even big specimen hunters get snapped off occasionally,

although they are probably loathe to admit it as it makes them look incompetent or unprofessional but it does still happen sometimes and if the 'big game hunters' don't get snapped off then it is because either 1. It happened to them once or more in the past and they learnt from it and took extra precautions I.e. stepped up the strength and quality of all their fishing tackle (rod, reel, line, wire leaders, knots etc.) or 2. They, above all others - due to their superior knowledge and experience of big, powerful fish, know full well not to underestimate the strength, speed and power of a big pike. They go 'heavy duty' so to speak. Don't go hunting twenty pound plus pike armed with 10 pound minus (due to the knot weakening the line.) Some line can stretch up to 30% but guess what happens when the line reaches the limit of it's inherent elasticity. Snap - bye bye fish.

Take care and take precautions: Buy good quality, reliable, strong line of an adequate breaking strain. Check your line for faults. Rub your finger tips up and down your line to check for faults, weaknesses or abrasions before you start fishing - clip off (with nail clippers) and discard any lengths of bad line. Check your knots, check the breaking strain/condition of your wire leaders, check the size, condition and sharpness of hooks and throw away and replace any rusty hooks or eyelets/ringlets. Use the right tools for the job in hand. Don't lose the fish of a lifetime for the sake of carelessness or laziness!

A wise man (Demosthenes) once said...

"LEAVE NOTHING TO CHANCE, WHICH CAN BE SECURED BY FORETHOUGHT AND SKILL"

Those are words to live by and words to fish by.

So, yeah, its not always your fault, sometimes it's just bad luck/ one of them things and breakages/snap offs do happen. Just do everything within your power to make sure that they don't happen to you! After all - it's disappointing (heart breaking) for you to lose what could very well be your pb (personal best) fish, and secondly - I don't want to be catching any 'deformed' fish!

It is easy to get overexcited when you connect with a big pike (especially if that pike has just come out of nowhere and swallowed you lure right in front of you!) You have to calm yourself down and remind yourself that a big pike has at least 3 or 4 good runs in it (if not 5 or 6). If you bear this in mind, stay calm, and take your time, then you are far more likely to land that big fish. Get overexcited, panic, (momentarily, forget everything that you ever knew about fishing in the heat of the moment) and try to bully in a big fish straight towards the bank and into the net and you may be sorry!

Fishing can be a super exciting sport but you must remember to always stay calm and take your time when 'playing' in a big fish... Although, it is the most natural thing to do, it doesn't help to respond to their energy - like for like. The fish may be going 'crazy' but the fisherman has to stay calm...

CHAPTER 2. THE PIKE - KNOW YOUR QUARRY

<u>RESPECT YOUR QUARRY</u>

It is amazing really...

If you encounter a deer, a squirrel, a hare, a rabbit, a fox, a badger, a frog, a toad, a rat, a water vole, a kingfisher, a heron or just about any truly WILD creature...

If you make any loud noise or sudden movement that alerts the animal to your presence then it will flee instantly, make its escape, and attempt to put as much distance as possible between itself and you and what is more, that is exactly what you would expect it to do!

How often do you see an angler fishing for carp, sat still in silence waiting patiently for a bite. Yet that self same angler, if he were fishing for pike, thinks nothing of snapping branches, stomping his feet, splashing water, talking loudly on his mobile phone, etc etc. Do these anglers not respect the pike? Do they not know that...

PIKE ARE TRULY WILD CREATURES...

They have excellent senses, they are extremely aware of their surroundings and that includes you! Wild animals or 'creatures' are NATURALLY AFRAID OF HUMANS - it is built into them (and pike are no different.)

Newsflash: A pike is a wild creature, as wild as a fox or a badger and sometimes just as wary. Once he is aware of your presence - half the game is up. The fish is not necessarily going to behave the way he would in his natural environment - if you were not there, or if he did not know that you were there. He has become conscious of your presence and this naturally leads to wariness/ caution on the fish's part. And it makes your job as a fisherman ten times harder...

THE SUBTLE SERPENT...

One year around 2006, I went on holiday with my dad in his mobile home. We drove here, there and everywhere, fishing all over the country. I cannot recall where I was, as this is nearly 20 years ago now. I was sat on my own, fishing on the bank of a good sized river. I was mostly hidden from view by the long, tall grass at the waters edge. I had a small gap in my peg, from which to look out across the water.

As I sat there on my own watching the river, a snake swam across the surface of the water, from my right to my left, it was weaving its way along the surface of the water. If I remember correctly it was swimming upriver. I didn't catch one single fish in that river, that day but as I told my dad later something more remarkable happened... I saw a snake with my very own eyes, for the first time in the wild and what is more interesting is that it saw me too! That snake had it's eye on me as much as I had my eye on him! I described it to my dad and he says that it could have been an adder! But then again, my dad reckons that he's better than me at fishing (and everything else!) and that he taught me everything I know!

I have since seen a second snake on the bank of the river Saw. Almost two decades later...

This time I am pretty sure it was an adder! There is a reason why

I am relating this little story...

It is the same reason why I have only seen 2 snakes in over thirty years of fishing... The reason is: Because snakes are the most stealthy of creatures...

Snakes are far more stealthy than us clumsy fishermen. A snake is renowned for it's stealth! Us fishermen need to learn to become more stealthy...

USE STEALTH...

Always use stealth to your advantage. Move slowly and tread lightly like you're treading on egg shells or walking on glass bare foot - Ninja style! The closer you get to the water's edge the more silent you should become...

Stay quiet. I know it is obvious but it is amazing how many people talk loudly, shout, stomp their feet, talk on their mobile phones, splash their feet or rods in the water, all of which is completely unnecessarily...

Being quiet costs us nothing and it can make all the difference between catching and blanking. Anglers must learn to treat pike with the same respect as carp!

A UNIVERSAL FISH

The pike (Esox Lucius) sometimes known as 'the northern pike' is an old fish. An ancient fish. A top end predator that has been around since time began. The pike and it's close relatives (muskellunge or muskies and pickerels) can be found all over the world. Pike are one of the most common, widespread fish on Earth. They can be found in England, Ireland, Scotland, Wales, Poland, Europe, Canada and America as well as other countries.

The pike is one of the most widely distributed fish on earth and is able to survive in almost any environment - even extreme cold. For this reason pike are often caught whilst ice fishing. They are an extremely durable, resilient and hardy species of fish.

THE PIKE IN HISTORY

In medieval times the pike was highly regarded as a food source. It was valued by no less than Edward I at double the price of salmon and ten times the price of cod. People have been fishing for them and eating them since time began.

At one time it was fashionable to catch them and have them preserved (stuffed) by taxidermists and placed in glass cases (like fish tanks) and mounted on the walls of houses. I have seen two or three such pike in real life. One was for sale in a fishing tackle shop! (the missus wouldn't even let me think about buying it!) Another one in a restaurant in Scotland near Loch Awe. There was also a stuffed trout on display!

They sometimes have them in pub's, restaurants, hotels etc to advertise the fish caught in nearby lakes (sometimes a very long time ago.) You have to ask yourself: How come nothing like that has been caught in more recent times? Is it because the water isn't as good today as it was back then? Or perhaps there's a lot less 'stuffing' going on these days.

THE PIKE'S NAME

The name 'pike' actually comes from a medieval weapon known as 'the pike.' The fish was named after this medieval spear due to them both sharing a similiar elongated, aerodynamic shape.

Esox Lucius is the pike's 'scientific' name. Interestingly enough, the name Lucius was at one time in history a popular name amongst king's and princes.

HOW THE PIKE HUNTS HIS PREY...

The pike is a super efficient hunter - an apex predator. His speed, accuracy, timing, and precision are second to none. He has the ability to swallow small prey whole.

The pike tends to hit larger prey side on at the shoulder/around the middle, or he chases them from behind and seizes/engulfs them in his jaws.

The pike swallows larger prey head first. He catches them (usually side on but sometimes 'head first') and crushes them in the vice like grip of his jaws until they are no longer able to breath. Once the pike is satisfied that they are dead (or as good as) and thus no longer able to escape from his jaws...

He expertly turns them little by little, bit by bit, inch by inch until they are in the perfect/optimum position to be swallowed. He then quickly swallows them head first.

The pike does not always wait until the prey fish is completely dead. Sometimes he turns them and swallows them head first whilst they are still alive but in a badly 'weakened' state or condition.

The pike is very skilful at turning prey and has an excellent grip (due to the 6 or 700 needle sharp, backwards pointing teeth in his mouth.) He is expert at making tiny 'micro' adjustments in the positioning of the prey trapped in his jaws. His success rate is very high but even so, the odd prey fish may 'miraculously' escape from the pike's jaws before or even during turning. The bigger the prey - the better his chances of escaping... This is the exception to the rule however. Most captured fish are done for once 'seized' and turned in this way. It is usually when the opportunistic pike's eyes are bigger than his belly that the 'larger' prey fish has the best chances of escaping/getting away.

In my opinion, the older and wiser a pike is: The more efficient a hunter she becomes... As she is able to draw on a wealth of experience of successful hunting and many 'interactions' with prey fish (in the past.) I have observed small pike up close, they have all the tools to hunt but nonetheless they are not born with experience and still have to learn to hunt. I believe a pike's 'success' rate improves with time, age and experience. They do indeed become more crafty and wily with time and even better at evading capture!

The pike is also a patient predator - this is part of the pike's hunting strategy. He can lie in wait for hours or even days on end just waiting for the perfect moment to strike...

AN EXPERT HUNTER...

I once watched a very large pike (on you tube) being filmed (at night) by an underwater diver...

There was a very large pike pursuing or hunting a smaller 'jack' pike under the cover of darkness. The large pike was aware of the smaller pike before the smaller pike seemed to be aware of her. In effect, the larger pike was actively hunting the smaller pike but the smaller pike (who was not really that small) was seemingly unaware of it. The large pike had slowly, very stealthily, creeped within range of her intended victim. The smaller pike at the very last moment seemed to become aware that something was sneaking up behind it and it was in danger or being hunted. The large pike stayed perfectly still (motionless) facing the smaller pike, perfectly positioned and 'primed' to strike. The smaller pike slowly, nervously turned around to face the threat but it was too late. With pin point accurate timing and devastating speed the large pike launched itself towards the smaller pike. The smaller pike too shot forwards at great speed in vain hopes of avoiding capture, but all to no avail. It simply launched itself like a willing victim straight down the other pike's throat. You could even hear a scraping sound as the smaller pike disappeared straight into the larger pike's mouth and directly into his belly. It was obvious that the large pike was an expert hunter. A wily, sly old fox against a young jack? It was no contest... The younger 'jack' never even stood a chance.

It was after watching this that I realised how clever and 'calculating' a big pike can be when hunting... How they are able to draw on past experiences. Selecting the right prey, choosing to wait until nightfall to make their move, and slowly, imperceptibly, closing the gap, and sneaking up on their prey from behind... The big pike made it look easy - too easy.

Seeing that video really made me think! You would think that a big pike would be too slow to catch a smaller, younger pike like that? Apparently not.

THE 'HIDDEN' HUNTER

The pike is a well camouflaged predator, just handle one and see its camouflage patterns come out. I once witnessed a pike's camouflage patterns come out and instantly 'appear' at the exact moment he pursued my lure! Not, after he was hooked, but before he 'struck' my lure! Now there's something to think about...

A pike's camouflage patterns can come out when they are being handled/unhooked and released back into the water. I have even had a pike let his mouth hang open, and flare his gills in order to make his head look bigger when I showed the pike to my excited, inquisitive dog. She likes to have a look and see what all the splashing and fuss is about.

This is a defensive response that pike have in the wild when they are approached by other pike that may see them as an easy meal. They make their heads look 'larger' in order to appear 'too big to eat.' The pike saw my dogs face and mouth hanging open excitedly, and interpreted her as yet another predator about to strike! The perch like the pike has bars or stripes down his sides in order to camouflage himself or blend into his surroundings. Again, the perch is both predator and prey in equal measure. It is commonly believed that a perch's stripes disappear when it dies? I have kept pike and perch in tanks for years... In fact, a perch's stripes can fade and disappear while it is alive and 'perfectly healthy.' You can have two perch in the exact same environment - one has very dark stripes and the other has very light stripes and both fish's stripes fluctuate between the two states depending on their mood... Regardless what the popular fishing magazine's tell you: There is a great deal about fish which we still do not know!

I have been keeping 'baby' or 'micro' pike in tanks on and off since 2010. I have also kept other species of native fish... I catch them in a landing or 'hand net' when they are tiny (about an inch in length or less!) One year I had four. From the youngest age, I have observed these tiny pike flare their gills in an attempt to look bigger and less appetising when they feel threatened or vulnerable. It is pure instinct for them to do so. It is quite funny to watch a pike that is smaller than a stickleback puff itself up (both pike do it) in the presence of another equally tiny pike! I have never had a tiny pike (or any pet pike) eat another one! There is a very good reason for this: If you have ever tried catching such a tiny pike then you will know what a feat this is and just how difficult it is to do. I am talking about pike so small that they can live on pet shop bought frozen (freeze dried) blood worms. A truly, tiny micro pike.

It took me years to figure out how to do this. I like to keep them for one year and then release them back into the wild - ideally in the exact same place that I caught them. I am not bragging or boasting but I have seen some pretty amazing things that other conventional fishermen are not privy to (as a consequence of observing predatory/coarse fish in tanks over the last 14 years.) More on this later...

THE PIKE'S 'ELUSIVE' NATURE

The pike is a very crafty fish. Craftiness is 'hardwired' into his brain as a survival mechanism to catch food. He knows how to hunt and catch his food, and is perfectly designed for it. He is both willing and able. The pike is both an opportunist predator and an active scavenger. He uses his eye sight, lateral line and neuromast system (those little dots on his face that look like teeth marks) to hunt by sight, feeling and vibration. He uses his sense of smell to scavenge dead fish off the bottom of the river/

lake bed. You could argue that his other role (a bit like my dog) is that of waste disposal unit.

THE PIKE'S SUPER SENSES...

THE PIKE'S VISION

I strongly believe that: The pike is primarily a sight feeder, he uses his eyes to hunt. The pike's eyes are very large and situated at the top and front of his skull. I have caught pike with eyes like sheep! If you look closely next time you catch a pike - you will notice that its eyes and especially its pupils are bigger than yours and that's when they are out of the water and in broad daylight! The pike has binocular vision, this means that he can primarily see what is in front of him and above him. This is for hunting fish, frogs, toads and small birds and mammals such as ducklings, moorhens, coots, water voles or rats. See the splashing and surface popping (top water) lures sections of this book. His large eyes also help him to see in low light conditions such as at dawn and dusk and also when water conditions are less than perfect such as in dark or muddy water or after heavy rainfall. A pike's eyes and their peculiar position on the top and at the front of his skull and looking downwards towards the tip of his snout, have been compared to a hunter looking down the sights of a telescopic rifle. The pike's strike accuracy really is quite incredible. Although they do still sometimes miss (a bit like a boxer) because they are usually aiming at a (sometimes fast) moving evasive target.

THE PIKE IS EVER CONSCIOUS OF THE FACT THAT HE IS BOTH PREDATOR AND PREY...

The pike's binocular vision helps him to spot birds of prey such as heron's, cormorant's, and kingfisher's which are his natural enemies. Being stationary for long periods of time does leave the pike quite vulnerable to predation from birds of prey as he represents less of a moving target to home in on.

Also, being a solitary fish rather than a shoal fish leaves him more isolated and easier to spot from above. Pike make themselves less vulnerable by seeking cover. They will lie beneath fallen trees/logs/tree branches, lilly pads, under willow trees, under banks, under bushes and beneath weeds, reeds, bull rushes, and generally hide anywhere they can. And having tried to find and catch them with a hand net I can tell you that they are very good at hiding/blending in! They have excellent camouflage to the extent that when I once caught a tiny one inch 'micro' pike I only just noticed it in my net and could easily have mistaken it for a small piece of weed! And that with 'trained' eyes. They are very sensitive to noise, sound and vibration and extremely evasive when they choose to be... The pike has an uncanny ability to hide itself in the most difficult to find places!

SENSE OF SMELL

The pike uses his incredible sense of smell to sniff out and scavenge dead fish off of the bottom. This is why sea fish such as mackerel and sprats make such incredible baits, just try to get the smell off of your hands and you will know what I mean. One time, me and my fishing buddy were having a lure/dead bait pike session whilst simultaneously using mackerel for a 'static' dead bait. We were taking off the old mackerel baits that were no longer well presented and tossing them in the water in front of us whilst we concentrated on lure fishing. Imagine our surprise when a pike completely ignored our lures and homed in on the smell of the dead mackerel in our swim. This has never happened before on a regular lure fishing session. Me and my friend both put it down to the mackerels overwhelming 'drawing power.' Try one for yourself - they really do stink! Catfish have at least as good a sense of smell as pike and most probably a much better sense of smell. They soon home in on dead mackerel put it that way! Other useful 'smelly' sea fish baits are sardines, herrings, and smelt.

THE PIKE'S SPEED AND CAPABILITIES

The pike is the fastest swimming freshwater fish on earth. Capable of reaching speeds of up to 40 kilometres an hour whilst in pursuit of prey or attempting to escape capture by larger pike or predators.

A long time ago, when I was a child, I once observed two pike, one in pursuit of the other... The first pike jumped clear out of the water (right in front of me) he leaped like a salmon, several feet up in the air. Incredibly the second pike performed the exact same manoeuvre, in hot pursuit of the first pike! Now, that is something that you don't see every day! I have also had a pike jump clean out of the water, right in front of me (at least 3 or 4 feet in the air) and take my lure in mid air when I was pulling it out of the water to recast it - I caught it too!

The pike pretends to be slow, sluggish and slothful but really he is the Ferrari of Fish - the fastest freshwater fish on earth. He is a very 'athletic' fish. In terms of concentration, sensory awareness, rapid acceleration, bursts of speed, split second timing and pin point accuracy - he has no equal. The pike likes to play the part of a harmless, docile fish, in order to fool his prey. The pike's slow movement is an act, a ploy that belies his true speed and capabilities. The pike is really capable of incredible bursts of speed and acceleration (up to 40 kilometres per hour) over a short distance of up to about 15 - 20 feet or 5 or 6 metres.

THE PIKE'S LIFE EXPECTANCY

The pike's age or the 'ageless' pike...

It was once thought that a pike could live for 250 years or even hundreds of years! We now know this to be untrue...

Realistically, a pike's maximum age in a perfect living environment is about twenty years. This is not the average age however. It is like the equivalent of a human being living to be 120 years old. The average fully grown, mature pike might realistically live to be 12 or 13 years old before dying of natural causes.

There are historically documented scientific records which show pike living to be 19 years old. I do not know of any records of any pike living to be 20 years old but that does not mean that they cannot live to be 20 years old or even older in the right conditions. It just means that (to my knowledge) none have been found, captured, or documented yet.

"THE FEMALE OF THE SPECIES IS MORE DEADLY THAN THE MALE."

THE PIKE'S SIZE

Ideal habitats for big (female) pike are trout reservoirs and large gravel pits.

It has been said that in the right living environment, and with an abundance of readily available food a female pike can realistically hope to reach 20 pounds in weight in just 5 years! The same pike could gain another 10 pounds and go on to reach 30 pounds in about another 3 years. That means that in the right environment a female pike could reach 30 pounds in weight in just 8 years! Now there's food for thought!

JACK PIKE

The Male or Jack pike are generally smaller than the Females and only grow up to about 10 or maybe 12 pounds in weight. The Female pike can, however, in the right conditions and food being readily available realistically reach up to and above 45 pounds in weight - Thus representing an awesome predator. There has been historically documented evidence of pike (in Ireland) reaching almost 100lb's in weight (96lb's to be precise.)

Fish this size are extremely rare and almost unheard of these days but that does not mean that they do not still exist!

Generally speaking: the larger the pike the rarer. The average sized pike is usually about three or four pounds in weight. Three and four pounders (jacks) abound everywhere. Large bodies of water such as the Norfolk Broads in England hold many big Females of twenty or thirty pounds and over in weight. Huge Scottish lochs and Irish loughs have the potential to turn up one of these Prehistoric monsters at any time... (If only there wasn't so much water to cover.) I have fished loch awe (a monumental task) which is twenty six miles long and drops off up to 300 ft deep in places. Sadly, it seems that in waters like these (a bit like the sea) fish are few and far between, with vast areas containing no or very few fish. However, if you are lucky enough to hit a fish it could very well be a big one...

Loch Lomond (where Fred Buller writes about getting snapped off and losing an enormous pike) is huge and seems to go on forever. When I was last there the water was atmospheric and dreamy... Crystal clear, perfectly flat, and as calm and as smooth as the silver reflection of a mirror.

Loch Ness is reportedly 750 ft deep and the stuff of legends. One of these days the British pike record will be broken, (I have faith) it's just a matter of being in the right place at the right time, with the right gear - that, being prepared and being lucky, being very, very lucky.

SPAWNING

Pike, like all fish spawn in the closed season - between mid march and mid june. They do not all spawn predictably at exactly the same time each year but different fish, in different waters, spawn at slightly different times each year (between march and june.)

Some would say that spawning times can be influenced by weather patterns and if we have an early or late summer.

You can tell when pike are spawning as you can see reeds and bullrushes moving about by themselves as the pike romp and frolick in the shallows.

The large female pike lays her eggs amongst the weeds and particularly bull rushes. The sticky eggs attach themselves to the stems of the reeds to stop the eggs from being washed down stream/river by the current.

CATCHING 'BIG' FEMALES AT RECORD WEIGHT...

Sometimes you can see and hear tell tale signs of splashing near the banks. If you are lucky enough to time it right, you can catch a big female pike at record weight and full of eggs. Pike are ravenous right before they spawn. If you time it wrong you will catch nothing as at spawning time pike (and other fish) are not interested in feeding as they are preoccupied with spawning. This is by design - when pike spawn - a big female (at record weight and loaded down with thousands of eggs) is chased and pursued by half a dozen or more smaller jacks intent on fertilising those eggs! If the big females were in hunting or feeding mode then these jacks would be nothing more than cannon fodder - easily caught and ate by a large, hungry female.

Nature equips the pike with an overriding desire to reproduce. This desire completely overrules the normally dominant desire to hunt and feed. After the jacks have served their purpose and the deed is done, the big female will have lost pounds in weight and now being long and lean become absolutely ravenous, rendering her easy to catch but nowhere near record weight. If you are lucky enough to time your fishing right after spawning - when the pike are back on the feed you can have a very successful days fishing although if you catch a big female at this time she will be long and lean where as if you had caught her a week earlier she would have been as fat as a pig.

It is a very wise man who knows exactly when the fish on the water he is fishing are spawning. Only experience can tell you that. Like I said, fishing at spawning time can be a complete waste of time so it is useful to have this knowledge to avoid wasted fishing sessions. Such knowledge is hard earned and hard won.

WHAT TO LOOK FOR WHEN EXAMINING PIKE...

Always check pike for: Unusual marks or distinguishing features such as being blind in one eye, obvious scars/bitemarks. This helps to differentiate between captures of different fish.

It is always useful to have a knowledge of (roughly) how many big pike there are in any given water and if a surprise specimen turns up out of the blue then so much the better.

Check for leeches as their presence on the pike will tell you that the pike are laid up resting on the bottom (which is quite often the case.) This helps you to determine at what depth to set your floats or fish your lures.

Always check the pike's mouth for fish or rodent tails hanging out of their throats (their last meal on display.) It helps to know what species are present in the water you are fishing and what the pike have been feeding on recently.

If a pike or catfish has a full hard belly then you know that they are feeding well. Some 'hardcore' fishermen will even put their hands down a catfish's throat and carefully pull out the contents to see what the fish are feeding on. Some of the more 'considerate' anglers will even carefully return the contents to the catfish's belly! Expect to get cut or grazed on your hands/ forearms if you carry out this practise.

It can also be worth checking pike's mouth's for old treble hooks/wire traces and broken rigs from snap offs as these things do happen occasionally - especially with kids/youths, and inexperienced anglers.

CHAPTER 3. THE PIKE'S PREDATORS

One of the biggest misconceptions about pike is that they are always the predator and never the prey. This is a completely unbalanced view and quite simply not true. If it was true then there would be thousands of pike swimming in every water. The truth is that the young pike is vulnerable and has MANY predators. The reality is that from the day that the pike eggs are layed and fertilized the pike are under attack. I have caught pike smaller than sticklebacks in my hand net! There are predators that will eat the pike's eggs (crayfish.) Pike, perch, trout, chub, catfish and zander (as well as others) will all view the young, immature pike fry as a nice, easy meal.

The young pike fry have to resort to eating each other in their race to reach maturity. Of the thousands of pike eggs that are fertilised in our waters every year, only a fraction of that figure will reach maturity. I would say that a survival rate of about 5% is a realistic, sensible estimate, although this will vary in each water and it could be from as low as 1 or 2% to as high as 10 or 20% depending on each water and it's own unique environment. Factor in otters and european mink which I have seen twice not a couple of miles from my home and the pike has got real problems.

The pike has to watch out for other fish from day one. This is why they tend to stay in the shallows seeking cover among the weeds and reed beds.

Any hungry fish, whether traditionally deemed as predatory or not is a threat to the baby pike. Any fish, that could potentially fit a pike into its mouth is a threat to the pike. All fish are predatory to some extent. Even a roach eating blood worms, maggots or worms could still be classed as exhibiting predatory behaviour. A roach may be silver and pretty but it still has to satisfy it's hunger and survival is it's number one priority.

It is historically documented that small silver fish such as roach have been caught on spinners. I myself, have once caught a (very) small silver fish on a spinner (not a chub.) I did not bother to look close enough to see what it was, I simply unhooked it and put it back in the water. I had bigger fish to fry as the saying goes...

BIRDS OF PREY

The pike is also vulnerable to kingfishers, herons and cormorants. Kingfishers will prey on baby pike. Heron often target pike due to them being a solitary and isolated fish that is immobile, and stationary for long periods of time. This marks them out as the perfect prey for the heron, who may occasionally attack and kill pike that are too big to eat. Pike and heron are natural enemies, The adult heron eat the young pike and I dare say that occasionally a large pike may return the favour and eat a small juvenile heron.

THE PIKE AND THE PERCH

The pike and the perch are natural enemies. They are both opportunistic predators, and ruthless cannibals. The perch will eat the small, young, vulnerable, and juvenile, baby pike without a second thought. The remaining pike that grow too big for the perch to eat, will prey on the perch and their young in return (as well as their own young.)

THE PIKE'S NEMESIS

The pike is his own Nemesis - his own worst enemy, his biggest rival and the number one threat to his own survival...

It is a true saying: **PIKE KEEP THEIR OWN NUMBER'S DOWN.**

Many a pike has been caught, with teeth marks on its head, side or tail from previous encounters with other pike where they have been grabbed. I make a point of checking all pike for bite marks when I catch them - just out of interest... It is always good to know what else is living, lurking and hunting in the immediate vicinity!

WHERE YOU CATCH ONE PIKE THERE ARE USUALLY OTHER PIKE...

<u>100% CANNIBAL</u>

Pike are both cannibal and predator in equal measure. They will have no qualms about eating their own young, from a young age - even pike of a very similiar size. Opportunistic hunters cannot afford to be fussy, or picky about food.

Nearly all predatory fish are cannibalistic. Many a perch has accidently been caught when livebaiting perch for pike. Trout eat trout. Big, old, male, brown trout are often called 'cannibal' trout. When they reach a certain size or age they become cannibals and survive by preying on their own species. My friend has a favourite Salmo trout imitation replica lure. He has caught specimen trout on it. He catches more trout on that lure than pike or any other species.

Back in the year 1999 or 2000, me and my friends were once fishing a deep pond full of perch. We caught several trout of two or so pounds each. We took them home for the pot and upon examining them they had bellies full of small (3 or 4 inch) perch!

<u>THE NATURE OF THE BEAST</u>

THE PIKE OR 'PREDATORS' NATURAL INSTINCT IS TO PREY ON THE WEAK AND VULNERABLE...

Fish live in a wild, primitive, dangerous world. Danger is lurking at every turn and around every corner. To a predatory fish it is dog eat dog - survival of the fittest. A pike is more concerned with its own survival than the survival of his or her young or the pike species as a whole. It is 'every fish for himself' and in this way they inadvertently ensure the survival of their own species.

To a pike, or any fish for that matter - their number one priority is survival, survival is paramount. That is why fish fight like tigers when hooked on rod and line - they realise that they are in danger and are still, as usual, just trying to escape danger and thus survive.

Fish live in a cruel, harsh, unforgiving environment where their first mistake may well be their last. I am not trying to exaggerate or to villainise the pike but the reality is that from the day it is born a pike is engaged in a fight for its own survival as are all fish in the wild. Pike and predators are selfish creatures. They always take the path of least resistance - the easy option. It's just nature... Fish eat fish. Pike eat pike, perch eat perch, trout eat trout, and so on...

10lb BREAM - CAUGHT ON LIVEBAIT!

Did you know that it has been historically documented that a fisherman of years gone by once caught a ten pound bream whilst livebaiting for pike! I cannot remember now what type of fish was being used for bait but I think that it was a roach or some sort of silver fish...

A 'BIG' PREDATOR HIDING IN THE SHADOWS...

(Witnessed by six people including myself.)

This was almost 20 years ago now... Back in June of 2004, I was spinning for pike on a large, deep lake. Or, as I like to call it 'paradise lake.' It was a cold, extremely windy day. This lake contained specimen pike, jack pike, specimen carp, specimen chub and perch as well as various other 'coarse' fish. My set up was a bit crude... I was using a one piece 6ft boat road. 13lb (catfish and zander) breaking strain line, a home-made wire trace and a 'modified' pike plug, which had a short (1 inch) bright orange head and a roughly 3 inches long white body. It sank very slowly and gradually dived (slowly) and wobbled from side to side enticingly as you retrieved it. Me, my brother, and some friends made our way to a likely looking (if somewhat neglected and overgrown) peg. (Those are usually the best ones.)

FISH (ESPECIALLY PIKE) 'THRIVE' ON NEGLECTED WATERS...

It was a grey and overcast day. I looked out onto the lake... The wind was blowing hard on the surface of the water. It didn't look very promising, it seemed that I had chosen the windiest day of the year! The water was nice and deep with a muddy brown, 'silty' bottom. There were patches of green weed on the surface and at mid depth. I aimed my lure and cast out, aiming for the corner of an island out in the distance. (I thought there may be some pike or perch there.) It looked 'pikey.' My lure hit the surface of the water, right on target, just off the 'corner' of the island. I began to reel in - nervous with excitement and anticipation. The orange and white plug I was using ('red head') had served me well in the past. I had already caught me 3 or 4 pike recently on this lake using said lure, so my confidence was high. My lure fluttered enticingly and began to sink to a good 3 or 4 feet down, in what seemed to be 8 - 10 feet of deep water. All of a sudden, a dark figure stealthily emerged from underneath the nearest corner bank of the island. It had a 'big' black silhouette and was swimming very quickly and aggressively in pursuit of my lure... "Do you see that?" Martyn said. "Yeah, I see it." Nicky said. "What is it?" Martyn said. "Can you see that?" I said, reeling in very carefully, hoping to fool whatever it was. "I can see that" said nick. "It looks like a huge trout" Martyn said. It's definitely got the colouring of a trout" I said. "But it's just too big and nobody has ever caught a trout in this lake before."

Whatever it was - was swimming closely behind my lure now, and I was having to speed up my retrieve so as the fish wouldn't get to 'scrutinize' my lure too closely and decide that it wasn't 'prey' after all. Luckily, I had cast out quite far and wouldn't run out of line on the retrieve - for a while yet anyway! My legs were almost shaking at the sight (and size) of what was clearly a large, aggressive 'unknown' predator approaching 3 feet in length and well into double figures in weight... All the while, this huge fish was swimming aggressively in pursuit of, and chasing my lure. I was concentrating like mad on making my lure seem 'alive' and 'swim' like a prey fish in distress... (I was the one in distress!) What if the big predator thought better of it, turned back and swam into his lair? What if he saw us? (All six of us.) What if I ran out of line? Meanwhile, the conversation or should I say 'commentary' went something like this: "What is it?" "I don't know." "It looks like a huge brown trout!" "No, it's too big and the wrong shape." "Well, it's not a pike." "No, it's definitely not a pike." "It must be a catfish." Somebody said. "Yeah, must be, it looks like one, it's very dark coloured and 'heavy set.' I had never caught a catfish at this time... Suddenly, it snapped at my lure and tried to 'engulf' the whole thing in one go! "Yes!" I exclaimed, and with split second timing - I struck hard - the fish was on! Suddenly, it turned tail and bolted off in the other direction! Luckily, my drag was set just right, otherwise I would have been snapped instantly! The huge fish was heading (or should I say 'steaming') off in the opposite direction, straight past the original island 'hole' that it had been hiding in. It was heading for an island far off in the distance, out in the middle of the lake. "No can do" I thought to myself, "or I'll run out of line!" I started to apply some 'pressure' to the fish. I used to joke that the the rod that I was using was made of titanium and "practically indestructable" - luckily! That old rod hardly acknowledged a fish - let alone bent - but it was bending and groaning under the strain and pressure of a huge angry fish! "Play it!" Said Martyn. "Play it!" "Don't lose it" screamed Nicky. All sorts of thoughts raced through my mind... "Would the line hold?" "What if it breaks?" "What on earth have I got on the other end of this line?" Gradually the fish began to tire and swim closer to the bank where I was standing. We all strained our eyes to see what it was through the 'ripply' surface of the wind blasted water. Closer and closer it came, it was big, it was black. "It's not a catfish," I thought to myself. "It's a carp!" Everyone screamed in unison. A carp on a pike plug! A mirror carp to be precise... This never happens I thought to myself. The odds of it happening were like one in a million! Or, once in a lifetime! But I (and 5 others) had seen it with our very own eyes! That mirror carp had 'stalked' my lure, chased it 'aggressively' and taken my plug ferociously and decisively like a big, black predator - hiding in the shadows, in deep water.

Using my lure fishing skills, and the advantage of 'reduced visibility' due to a strong wind on the surface of the water... I had done the seemingly 'impossible.' I had caught a 15 lb Mirror Carp on a modified 'red head' pike plug...

PREDATORY CARP

A carp is not 'classed' as a predatory fish. Nobody would think to fish for carp on lures or deadbait. Yet I caught a fifteen pound mirror carp on a red and white 'modified' pike plug, I saw both the carp stalking my lure and the take (a very aggressive take) and the fish was lip hooked, as photographed and witnessed by six people.

That was over twenty years ago now and I was pleasantly surprised at the time to say the least. My local tackle dealer was not surprised. Two of his customers had similiar experiences when pike fishing. One of them caught a carp of about 18lb's on a sprat, the other caught a carp of a similiar size using a 'rubber neck' jelly lure or shad. The last time I saw him (said tackle dealer) he showed me a photo of a common carp (unsure of the exact weight now but probably double figures - ten to fifteen pounds or so) caught on a bright orange, 6 inch, minnow type, shallow diving pike plug. My sister had a pond on her back garden, she found a frog, she tossed it into the water and (to her surprise) one of her ornamental gold fish slurped it up!I have even seen a carp drag under a baby duckling on the internet on youtube... Don't believe me? check it out for yourself...

A BELLY FULL OF FISH!

I heard another story in my local tackle shop. A very serious carp fisherman found a very large, dead carp (about thirty pounds in weight) in a fishery. He asked the owner of the fishery what he should do with it. The owner said "you can do whatever you like with it - just get it out of the water!" The carp specialist fished it out and out of pure curiosity decided to gut the carp and see what it had been eating... Imagine his surprise upon discovering that it had a belly FULL of small fish!

ALL OR MOST FISH ARE BY NATURE - PREDATORY - TO A GREATER OR LESSER DEGREE.

BORN PREDATORS

The bigger they get the more likely fish are to become predatory. Although some fish such as pike, trout and perch are born predators from a very young age.

Once and only once - I saw a shoal of little, tiny 'minute' silver fish (roach I am guessing) about a centimetre in length each (if that) being terrorised by half a dozen pike of about the same size. The 'newborn' pike were lined up just on the outskirts of this 'micro' shoal periodically launching themselves at the roach trying to pick them off, one by one. I stood and watched them for a while - amazed at what I was witnessing! I never saw one of the baby pike catch a baby roach (or chub or whatever.) So I can only imagine that these tiny, baby pike were just beginning to learn to hunt in a primitive, over eager, trial and error fashion. Nobody had to tell me that what I was witnessing was something rare and very rarely ever seen by fishermen. I have only ever seen it once in my life and completely by chance - right time, right place, on a small local river probably just days after spawning had taken place.

It is a mistake to think that only fish like pike, trout or zander eat fish. Just because you can physically, visibly see a fish's teeth does not make it any more predatory than a fish whose teeth you cannot see. Such as a chub, perch or even a carp where you cannot see their teeth but believe me they are there, and what is more - they are impressive. It just so happens that certain species of fish's teeth are not visible as they are located in the back of the throat. Even so, carp and other coarse fish eat a protein rich diet and feed on other living creatures (be that insects) from a very early age. If it were not so then these species of fish would not be able to hunt and eat crayfish which have hard shells.

CATFISH AND PIKE...

You will by now no doubt have heard many times that the pike is the 'apex' predator... Well, he isn't. Not when there are big catfish about! The presence of big catfish in any pike water leads to more competition for food for the pike. And potentially he is no longer at the top of the food chain anymore - the catfish is! It is a simple fact. The fish with the biggest mouth, that grows the biggest, the longest and the heaviest is the 'top' dog.

I have fished several lakes that contain both pike and catfish. On one of these waters... The biggest pike that I have ever seen, or heard of being caught is about ten pounds in weight! The biggest catfish was AT LEAST four times that size! On one of the other pike and catfish lakes the biggest pike is only about six pounds! The ten pound pike on the first lake has been caught more than once over several years but had not grown any bigger and seemed to have deteriorated and was in worse condition the second time it was caught! It is possible that the ten pound pike was a male and so had reached the upper limits of his realistic maximum weight. He was able to 'live' among the bigger catfish without being predated upon but I would not say that these pike were 'thriving' the way they would be if they were not competing with the catfish for food! If the catfish were removed or 'not there' in the first place, then these pike would be doing alot better. That is just the way it is!

I have seen examples on other waters where all or the majority of the pike are removed and the other predators in the water (perch, trout and chub) all start to thrive within a few short years and become 'specimen' fish.

Ever heard the saying "nature hates a vacuum?" If you took away all the chub then the perch might thrive or benefit from the chub's absence... (Less competition for food.) If you took away all the perch then the trout might thrive... But then again all these species of fish feed on each others young so it may not be that simple...

CHAPTER 4. THE PIKE'S PREY

<u>HOW THE PIKE SELECTS HIS PREY</u>

The pike or predator will target a fish or creature that is:

1. Alone, isolated or seperated/alienated from the shoal. (Which is why they are so partial to lures, plugs, spinners and 'live' baits) because they swim (alone) in an 'injured' fashion. As if they were physically unable to keep up with the shoal...

2. Out of its element or not in its usual or 'preferred' natural environment (such as a small mammal, rodent or amphibian.) Basically any small creature that lives on land as well as in the water such as a small mammal - rat, water vole, shrew, mouse, bird (or amphibian) frog, toad, newt, lizard or snake. Or other i.e. an insect.

3. Injured/wounded - possibly from a recent pike encounter.

4. Sick, ill or diseased - also from a recent pike attack, bite or festering open wound, that has become infected. A pike can tell if a fish is sick, ill or diseased by visible bite marks or wounds, it's 'wobbly' swimming pattern or by it being on it's own - isolated and unable to keep up with the rest of the shoal.

This is why pike target lures or plugs that imitate fish because A. the pike interpret them as fish that are alone or have strayed/ seperated from the safety of the shoal and B. They appear ill/ unhealthy due to the perceived wobble or off-balanced unusual swimming patterns. They stand out like a man with a limp!

IN THE WILD...

SMALL 'PREY' FISH DO NOT SWIM ALONE, THEY HERD TOGETHER IN SHOALS FOR SAFETY AND SECURITY. OTHERWISE, THEY GET PICKED OFF...

For prey fish there is indeed (relative) safety in numbers. This is why pike go for plugs, because of their wobbly, uneven and irregular swimming pattern or style which is designed to represent a sick, ill, diseased or dying fish. Because they don't swim in shoals! they swim alone - with me reeling them in at the other end! But that's not what the pike sees...

5. Small, young, naive or juvenile - A pike knows that smaller or younger fish are more vulnerable and naive than older, 'wiser' fish. In my experience fish do indeed become wise especially chub, perch, trout, carp and pike. They become harder to catch, for all predators - including fishermen, whom fish view as yet another potential threat or predator.

For example take small perch - they are very naive, over aggressive and easy to catch but big perch are shy and much more wary. A small Jack is also naive, overaggressive and easy to catch but a twenty or thirty pounder has been around a long time, and is wiser, and much harder to catch.

Fish do indeed learn from previous encounters, such as being chased or grabbed by pike or other predators (a 'stressful' and not very pleasant experience for any fish.) Or being caught on lures and released back into the wild.

In my experience a Jack will go for the same bait or lure several times (usually until he's caught) even though something doesn't 'feel' quite right. A big pike won't. He'll hit it once and if there is anything at all 'fishy' about it - such as: a fisherman in the vicinity, some nutter shouting at the top of his voice "I'm in" (me - back in the day!) or a rough, hard strike, or the big pike getting his head 'pulled off' by an over enthusiastic fisherman etc then that pike will be off like a shot and probably won't bite again that day. If he hits the lure and it doesn't quite feel right (too hard to be food) or he feels the tell tale prick of a sharp hook... Then he will reject the bait or lure and very rarely be tempted to bite again that day. Remember: Big pike don't get to be 'big and old' by being dumb!

6. Big and overconfident. Such as another pike or predator of similiar size. When fish reach a certain size they become specimens. They have reached maturity and become much less vulnerable to predation, than they were when they were younger and smaller. They have become less vulnerable - however, not immune to attack. even though they are less vulnerable - they are still vulnerable to a large enough predator. Imagine a lake that contained perch of four pounds, chub of five pounds, or trout of five pounds. All formidable predators in their own right. Now imagine a lone thirty pound pike... Its a whole different ball game.

These other fish may 'see themselves' as predators rather than prey but to a thirty pound pike all these other fish are all 'fair' game. This is what gives a really big predator the edge - the element of surprise. His prey may not realise that they have any predators left!

There have been documented cases of thirty pound pike taking pike in the region of six pounds and above.

There is one documented case of a huge pike being caught with a ten pound Salmon in his belly!

There is another documented case of a huge pike being caught with four adult ducks in her belly!

7. Unable to see the pike or predator. For example: a creature swimming on the surface, above and in front of the pike. Such as a small mammal, rodent, water vole, shrew, rat or mouse.

A frog, toad, newt or lizard. A large or small snake swimming on the surface of the water. A small bird that has fell out of a nearby nest. Baby ducklings, ducks, coots, moorhens, divers, baby herons or other waterfowl are all especially vulnerable to pike attack under the cover of darkness. See the 'bird eating monster' section of my book for a true testimony of a pike eating waterfowl.

8. Vulnerable in water or a technically inferior, slower, less mobile swimmer. Such as: A bullhead or crayfish, a frog, toad or newt. A water vole, shrew, rat, rodent or small mammal or small waterfowl such as: A baby duckling, moorhen, coot, diver or baby heron.

9. Extremely vulnerable or 'helpless' in water. Such as an insect that has fallen from an overhanging tree or a lobworm washed in by the rains and rising water levels. Or a small bird that is unable to fly and has fallen from her nest in a nearby, overhanging tree.

10. Dying or on it's last legs. Again, possibly due to the stress or trauma of a previous pike attack. The pike may simply be following up on a previous pike attack or simply waiting for a chance to finish off prey from a previous, earlier encounter. A bigger, slower pike may be hoping to swoop in and capitalize on the work of a smaller, faster, more 'agile' pike. This is what lions do to cheetahs in the wild, they let them catch something to eat, the cheetah being lighter and faster, and then they simply take it off them, the lion being bigger, more powerful and more dangerous than the cheetah. This all fits in with 'using economy of effort' and opportunist hunting and feeding.

A fish may have been 'deep hooked' by an unsupervised child, or an incompetent fishermen who forgot to watch his float/or strike and then pulled the fish's guts out (unhooking it) and released the poor fish back into the water in that terrible state (it does happen.) Or a fish that is dying of disease, old age or natural causes.

11. Dead fish. Smaller predators such as trout, perch and chub can easily be caught on floating, dead sticklebacks, or minnows, or indeed young fry or parr of any species, when and where there is enough competition for food.

Large predators such as specimen or double figure pike often turn scavenger because scavenging is easier than hunting. But make no mistake about it they are still 'super efficient' hunters and can still move or 'strike' very quickly!

Do not be deceived: The bigger the pike is - the bigger her tail is and the bigger the fin's surrounding her tail. The bigger the pike - the more muscle there is to propel her forward with one powerful swish of that huge muscular tail.

All predatory fish may occasionally scavenge a dead fish that is floating down stream or lying on the bottom but pike are particularly partial to scavenging. Again, this ties in with economy of effort or maximum reward for minimum effort or energy expenditure.

Note: If 2 pike home in on the same dead or dying prey fish then 1 of 2 things will usually happen...

1. Usually the bigger, more dominant pike will take precedence and take the initiative to see off the smaller (inferior) pike. Then he will either eat his meal where it is or swim off to his lair, turn it and swallow it head first.

2. The other turn of events is as follows: The smaller or inferior, naive, hungry pike may in his haste and foolishness, or being overeager and suffering from tunnel vision shoot in quick and grab the 'easy meal' (usually to his detriment.) The bigger pike will then usually respond by grabbing the smaller pike and eating him. Sometimes if the pike are a similiar size, then the smaller one may get away with it (occasionally.) One pike may chase, grab or attack the other in spite of the fact that he is not

physically big enough to eat him. This may be due to predatory instinct, hunger, desperation or territory. Pike will often try to eat things that are too big if they are handed to them on a plate just because they cannot resist an easy meal. I have reeled big carp and bream in to the bank and watched pike follow them in 'desperate' to eat them, even though it was a physical impossibility (wrong size and shape) for them to do so.

A FISH THAT WILL SUFFER NO RIVALS

According to a pike or predatory fish, the easiest way to get rid of your rivals - is to eat them! Less competition for food you see, and you don't have to watch out for over-ambitious young upstarts, climbing the ranks and trying to 'muscle' in on your action or take the bread off your table.

Predatory fish are very territorial, there is a 'pecking order' and if you don't comply you will most likely end up getting eaten! If you have ever observed trout in the wild, in a river or stream, then this is what you will have noticed: The biggest trout takes pride of place, in the best feeding spot at the head of the river or stream. A medium sized trout slots in nicely behind him and then a small trout lies at the back, happy to accept the meagre, slim pickings or left overs! The medium sized trout NEVER overtakes the big trout or the big trout will see him off.

If the smallest trout had the 'downright audacity' to swim in front of the medium sized trout then the medium sized trout would attack him! and if the small trout was foolish and presumptious enough to swim in front of the big trout then the big trout would definitely eat him! This is how the pecking order works. I have seen it in real life many times. I was pike fishing once in a small river, using a blue, white and yellow 6 inch, shallow diving, minnow type pike lure called an Abu Garcia Tormentor... They are very, very good by the way, they have a great rolling, side to side wobbling motion. As I was reeling in my lure, a brown trout of about 3 or 4lb's in weight attacked my pike plug right in front of me!

Another time I caught a common trout of about one pound on a small silver spinner and promptly released him upstream. He swam directly into the lair of a bigger trout of about two pounds who immediately chased him off, back down stream. This is the pecking order in action.

It's different with pike. A pike could be prowling around a river, pond or lake looking for a good hidy hole, resting place, or ambush point. "that looks like a good ambush point" he thinks to himself (just humour me.) When he unwittingly stumbles upon a bigger pike already laid up in that spot. "Whoops - too late!" He has been grabbed - probably headfirst and swallowed whole! You see, a pike can swim (forwards) very quickly but only swim backwards slowly! There is no room for error when you're swimming with the sharks (freshwater sharks - or crocodiles.)

GREEDY JACKS...

I once caught a small Jack pike of about two feet or so in length (four or five pounds) on a spinner. I opened his mouth and looked down his throat, to see what his last meal was (as is my usual custom.) There was a large tail hanging out of the back of his throat. Me and my fishing buddy got into a little debate... "What's that?" said my friend. "Another pike" I replied. "No, it's not" he said "it's a big roach." "Okay then, lets have a look" I said. With that, I pulled my plyers out of my pocket and began to slowly retrieve the tail of the pike's last meal. It was indeed, another pike. I said "it's almost the same length as the one that ate it!" The pike that was eaten was about 2 or 3 pounds in weight and was almost as long as the one that had eaten it! The only difference was the girth and maturity. And even after eating a meal that must have represented at least 50% of his body weight, the greedy guts still couldn't resist my spinner!

CHAPTER 5. IN PURSUIT OF ESOX LUCIUS...

THE MAJESTIC PIKE

A peasant seeks a fortune with not a penny in his pocket,
He searches for treasure but not a jewel or a locket.
The common man seeks royalty as he wanders off alone,
Whilst the queen in her palace, sits on her throne.
For what he must do, he must do on his own...
It's man versus beast - hook versus bone.
Driven by passion, forged by desire,
With red hot intensity, burning like fire.
He'll walk many miles, he'll pay any price,
She's the queen of all fish - worth all sacrifice.
He stands alone amongst men - with an eagles eye,
But she's as subtle as a serpent gliding swiftly by...
And who shall triumph and who will fail?
Is victory in man's hands? Or in fishes tail?
It's a test of cunning, of stealth, and of skill,
It's a game of guile, of wit and of will.
A skilled hunter, a master, a steely eyed son,
But the beauty of a mystery is that she answers to no one.
He hunts the monster amongst the reeds and the leaves,
But finds nothing but the shadow of a whisper of a thief.
And where may I find her? and where does she lie?
The merest trace of an echo - a glint in your eye.

An impossible riddle - where does she hide?
In front and behind and on either side.
His rod is invincible - no fish has broke it's back,
But alas many times his line has gone slack.
His hooks are sharp, his line never fails,
But her strength is her speed, her power her tail.
Her speed is like lightning - an arrow in flight,
She strikes her prey at the speed of light.
She wears her camouflage like a perfect disguise,
And hides in the shadows - invisible to the eye.
He summons all his energy - the full intensity of his mind,
But alas you cannot catch, what you cannot find.
His eyes pierce the water and lay everything bare,
But no man can catch what simply is not there...
Beneath the dark shadows of towering trees,
My queen answers to no one - least of all me.
I think of nothing but her as I sharpen my hook...
Always seeing her but never finding her, wherever I look.

THE MAD PIKE MAN

Ireland: The year 1880...

John Bickerdyke (famous fishermen, pike fisherman and author) gives an account of meeting an obsessed pike fishermen who if I'm completely honest kind of 'reminds me of me' but much, much worse and much, much further along in his obsessive 'dedication.' On his fishing travels John Bickerdyke discovered a mad englishman who had moved to Ireland to live, in pursuit of a forty pound pike. This mad (or extremely dedicated - depending how you look at it) gentleman had lived in Ireland for almost fifty years, fishing almost every day and (you guessed it) always for pike. Now that is dedication! If he had written a book on pike fishing then I would have been first in the queue to buy it!

In the story, John Bickerdyke witnesses the old man weighing "the biggest pike Bickerdyke had ever seen." The big pike tipped the scales at thirty five pounds but the old man was sincerely disappointed. Nothing less than forty pounds would do! With this the old man fainted and his wife informed Bickerdyke that he had not eaten for a full two days! I told you he reminded me of me! Now, I am dedicated (borderline obsessed) with pike fishing and catching big pike and sometimes I do go to extremes. I have gone without food or drink for many a full 'exhausting' day but never two days in a row! The old man had made a bet with his friends back in england that he would catch a forty pound pike and vowed that he would not return to england until he had done so...

This old pike fisherman tried all the Shannon loughs, Corrib and Cullen. He caught many pike but none that weighed forty pounds. The biggest pike that the old man had caught at the time that Bickerdyke met him, after a lifetime of pike fishing, was thirty five pounds and that was the biggest pike that the old man had ever seen caught anywhere, by anyone and that after almost fifty years spent in pursuit of Esox Lucius!

The old man told Bickerdyke that he had at last found the whereabouts of a "truly monstrous pike, a pike as big as a calf, in a deep, reedy lake." When Bickerdyke expressed an interest in joining the old man to catch the monster pike the following morning the old man's eyes narrowed with suspicion . "But then you might catch him and not I" he said. There ensued a long silence. The old man did not wish to give away the location of a fish that he had spent 50 years and the best part of his life trying to catch.

During the night he feigned madness and whispered in Bickerdykes ear "hang me if I don't believe that you are a pike. I'll have a hook into you tomorrow morning." Bickerdyke concluded that the old man had been driven mad by his long quest to capture a giant pike. Maybe he had or maybe he was just smart and realised his mistake (telling a fellow pike fisherman about the fish of a lifetime - located not a quarter of a mile from his house) and didn't want anyone else coming between him and his prize. Bickerdyke took the hint and fled at first light. He never returned to the old man's home.

The moral of the story is that after nearly fifty years of fishing Irish rivers and Loughs almost every day, he never caught a pike of over thirty five pounds!

Now tell me that luck doesn't come into it!

YOU HAVE GOT TO BE IN THE RIGHT PLACE AT THE RIGHT TIME...

Fully prepared, highly skilled and very, very lucky...

THE HARDEST PART OF CATCHING BIG PIKE OR ANY BIG FISH FOR THAT MATTER IS FINDING THEM.... Just ask a sea fishing skipper!

Location, location, location as they say or as I like to say **"you cannot catch what is not there."** No matter how good you are.

The other moral of the story is this...

Perhaps the old man never was mad but after disclosing his hard earned and hard won secret's immediately realised his mistake in revealing the location of his dream fish to a passionate, fellow pike fisherman. Lets not forget that he had been on the trail of a forty plus pound pike for the best part of fifty years! He may not have realised at first that Bickerdyke was a serious pike fisherman and thus inadvertently let his guard down. As time went on he realised that Bickerdyke was a serious pike fishermen and thus saw him as a potential threat that could come between him and his prize. Upon realising his mistake he feigned madness in order to frighten his young protege off the scent and guess what? It worked, and who knows? Perhaps that mad (I like to think of him as extremely dedicated) old pike fisherman did go on to catch a forty pound plus pike as big as a calf. Who knows? It was his lifetime's ambition after all, but one thing's for sure... I bet he came pretty close (closer than anybody else of his time) and if he didn't I bet he still enjoyed himself trying and it wouldn't have been for lack of effort and dedication on his part! I just wish that he had written a book documenting his pike fishing exploits over those fifty long years. That would have been well worth a read!

BE WISE: DO NOT REVEAL YOUR PRECIOUS SECRETS TO OTHERS...

DO NOT CREATE RIVALS FOR YOURSELF, LEST THEY STEAL YOUR THUNDER AND YOUR GLORY (AND YOUR PIKE.)

I have a confession to make now... If I go in a fishing tackle shop and see a picture of a big pike on the wall... The first thing I do is study the photograph very closely to see if there are any obvious visible landmarks or distinguishing features (in the background) which enable you to pin point exactly where the fish was caught...

Sometimes you can tell, and if you are able to tell then that little clue or tidbit can save you a lot of reconaissance work. I am after all these years a 'wily old fox.' And I suggest that you do the same... I on the other hand do my very best to "not let the left hand know what the right hand is doing" if you see what I mean... (I usually try to hide the 'exact' location of where any of my trophy fish are caught.)

I have another confession to make... I am speaking from personal experience here. I once made the mistake of creating a 'rival' for myself. He went on to be a very well trained, hard working, clever, resourceful rival. He was very dedicated, he put in a lot of hours and it paid off for him. He caught a very large pike on one of my favourite lakes. I am glad for him. If anyone deserved to catch a pike like that it was him, but I still can't help thinking... 'I wish I had caught that fish!'

The story of the mad (dedicated) pike fisherman who spent nearly fifty years of his life fishing almost every day for pike is a great story.

It just goes to show what a wonderful, glorious, fascinating, mysterious, absorbing, all engrossing pastime pike fishing really is and just how deep into this obsession you can be drawn. If you let yourself...

Just think of it:

FIFTY YEARS - HALF A CENTURY!! SPENT FISHING NEARLY EVERY DAY AND ONLY EVER FOR PIKE!!!

It's amazing when you think about it! I love it. I wish I had a friend like that! Imagine the things he has seen over those fifty long years and all the stories he could tell...

Imagine what he might have found in that thirty five pounders belly! Imagine all the things he could have taught you about pike and pike fishing. He wouldn't let you down if it was raining a bit would he? Oh well back to reality...

I have been fishing for over thirty years now, so you'll just have to listen to me droning on for a bit longer! I don't mind revealing all my secrets...

Well most of them anyway (second thoughts) well some of them at least, a few... As long as I don't catch you fishing on my patch, in my favourite peg (the secret one) come saturday morning...

THE FISHERMAN AND THE PIKE

On a summer's day, beneath a golden sky,
He made his way to the water's side,
With a bag on his back and a rod in his hand,
He trod a trail of rock and sand.
With army camouflage and wellingtons to his knees,
He made his way through the bushes and trees,
With a smile on his face and a glint in his eye,

He crept like a fox to the waters side...

The sun cast reflections of towering trees,
The wind kissed the water as cool as a breeze.
With patience he threaded his line through each eye,
With the care of a spider in pursuit of the fly.
He scanned the water like a hawk in the air,
A few rocks and logs, a fish here and there.
He searched the water - as though a gold mine,
Amongst the weeds and reeds, he searched for signs.

A little downstream amongst the leaves and reeds,
He saw a dark shadow below a willow tree,
With a familiar form that you could not forget...
She was black as the night - a ghostly silhouette.
She lay motionless beneath the roots of the bank,
She was long and lean like a torpedo shank,
She was large and lazy and lurking about,
Green as the grass with a mean ugly snout.

He felt the excitement at the bottom of his belly,
That made his legs shake, and wobble like jelly,
The ugly face, the evil eye, teeth and jaws of massive size,
The freshwater crocodile - a glorious prize.
He searched through his bag, what should he pick?
A golden blade from his box of tricks,
The perfect imitation of wounded prey...
Go right ahead, make my day...

His hooks were sharp as a two edged sword,
His line as strong as invisible cord.
He cast his lure some way down stream,
It plopped in the water and spun like a dream.
It flashed with colour like a star in the sky,
But would it catch the monsters eye?
His hands are shaking, it's almost there...
Preparing to enter - the dragons lair...

Moving closer and closer... Right past her nose...
Her head's turning, her interest grows...
She's drifting out, she's giving chase...
His heart's racing at a terrific pace,
She hits it like an arrow that shoots through the air,
Then turns to sneak back into her lair.
he strikes at once - his rod is bowed...
The big girl runs - it's a heavy load!

She tugs, then thrashes and leaps into the air,
He steps into the water - she's fighting like a bear!
She turns and runs, his reel is screaming!
This can't be happening - he must be dreaming!
She's sailing off now, she's stripping away line...
He takes a deep breath and hopes everything's fine,
She breaks the surface, she's tail walking now!
Such awesome power! - Wow! - Just wow!

Oh no! What's happened? His line's gone slack!
He can't believe it! - She's swimming back!
he's turning his reel handle - as fast as he can!
It's man versus crocodile - brute versus man.
He's reconnected - the fish is still on!
It's all at stake now - a battle to be won.
She flares her gills and thrashes her head,
He's piling on the pressure but the fish feels like lead!

She's tiring now, she's laying on her side...
Victory never tasted sweeter, he's swelling with pride.
She's swimming towards the net, get in there my son!
He's stole the glory - his job is done.
he weighs her on the scales - ten, fifteen, twenty!
That'll do nicely, a twenty's just plenty!
he sets up the camera and does a quick pose...
A couple of quick snapshots and back the beauty goes...

STALKING RIVER/CANAL PIKE, PERCH, TROUT & CHUB

It has been my custom for as long as I can remember...

To walk up or down river or canal. Looking, searching, scouring and scanning the water for any visible signs of big, predatory, 'native' species of fish. I have trained myself to do this from my schooldays and can easily spot at a glance - what the casual, 'untrained' eye would miss...

I know where to look and I know what to look for. For a start, river fish always face upstream... Sometimes, what you are looking for and the easiest thing to spot is a shape, shadow, or silhouette. Other times, it is the subtle movement of a fish's fins 'flickering' or moving ever so slightly to hold it's position in the water against the current. Pike, for example, have relatively large fins which they use to hold their position in strong currents or fast flowing water. The most obvious fins to spot moving are the pike's pectoral fins or tail fin. I know from observing pike and perch in tanks: The pike uses the pectoral fins to steer himself left or right or hold his depth or position in the water. Likewise, he uses his tail fin to propel himself forward or hold his position against the current.

If you see a fishy or 'pikey' shape or silhouette in the water but you are still unsure. (Sometimes, it is just a shadow, some weed, or the side of a rock.) Look for the tell tale signs of micro-movement in the fish's fins. If you can clearly see fins - then it is definitely a fish, and it is time to take action... Cast out your lure, sprat, worm or bait. There are two ways to do it:

1. cast your sprat, worm or deadbait right in front of the fish's nose and either let it sink enticingly to the bottom or start reeling it in towards you slowly and enticingly.

2. Cast over the top of the pike, trout, chub or whatever it is and reel your lure or sprat slowly past the fish... Oh, and hold on tight. Boom - you're in business.

STALKING CARP...

I have even stalked large (lake and pond) carp using the same method or technique... Being a predator specialist, I like to roam, stalk, or actively 'hunt' fish. So, using the same principles, I simply walk around the banks of the pond/s lake/s I am fishing as slowly, quietly, stealthily and imperceptibly as I physically, humanly can... Stealth is the name of the game...

When I have successfully sneaked up on a carp which is (hopefully) facing the other direction. I then, cast out my bait - a large lobworm, piece of bread, boilie or whatever. As sneakily, or stealthily, as humanly possible...

I don't cast the bait right on top of the carp (so as to 'spook' him) but in front of him, a few feet away, but directly in his field of vision. Then I immediately duck down low to the ground, as low as I can get without losing sight of my bait and the fish.

If I spot a fish before he sees me and the fish is facing towards me then I will wait until the fish is facing the opposite direction (or out of line of sight) before aiming and delivering my cast...

Now, You have to remember: I am in full army camouflage gear. Not a bright red or orange T shirt! Anyhow, stalking has accounted for a fair few decent, double figure, carp. My biggest 'stalked' carp is about 15 pounds. And, one of my close fishing buddies has had the same type of success - carp to about 15 pounds proactively stalked. The difference is the time factor... If you can successfully stalk a carp (or any fish) you can have him on the hook or on the line pretty quick! It definitely saves time. You can succeed at this first time but it may take a bit of practise...

LONG RANGE FREELINING

Another sneaky trick I came up with is what I call 'long range' freelining. When I was a kid, I used to fish a river that ran under a double arched sandstone bridge into a private lake or fishery.

This was the type of 'exclusive' fishery that was "membership by invitation only." The lake was a natural 'river fed' fishery surrounded by barb wire and high fences. It cost thousands to join and the rumour was that there was only about 15 members (mainly old duffers) at any one time.

NECESSITY IS THE MOTHER OF INVENTION

Anyhow, there were some good chub on the other side of that sandstone bridge and I needed a stealthy way to catch them... I came up with this: Instead of using an ordinary float (too obvious.) I would rest a lobworm bait on top of a large leaf and let the leaf drift down river under the arches of the sandstone bridge and on into the lake. When the big leaf reached it's intended destination, I would give the rod tip a little flick and drop my freelined worm hookbait right into the chub's midst. I had some nice chub out of that swim! Luvly jubbly!

ESSENTIAL GEAR FOR PIKE AND PREDATOR FISHING

Multi (unhooking) tool/long-nose forceps/pliers. Plenty of wire traces/wire leaders - preferably long ones (at least 12 inches long.) A wire trace 'tube' for storage. Plastic lure/plug compartmentalised boxes with flip lids. Treble hooks (preferably barbed or at least 'micro' barbed in various sizes - 4, 6, 8 and 10. Large single hooks long shanked, circle hooks, or sea-fishing style hooks. Some size 12 or 14 regular or 'long shanked' hooks for large worm baits. Small hooks such as size 16 for catching 'live' baits. Army/camouflage trousers with lots of big, handy pockets for storing things. Light-weight summer trousers or warm winter trousers. Lures, plugs, spinners and spoons with plastic storage containers or at the very least 'hook guards.' Pike floats, cigar shaped floats, bubble floats etc. Weights/ledger bombs (optional.) Waterproof boots, wellington boots or thigh waders. Polarised glasses for seeing through surface glare. Various deadbaits - frozen or defrosted. A fishing rod (and a spare fishing rod.) A fishing reel (and a spare fishing reel.) A large spool of good quality spare line of at least 12 pounds breaking strain. Some wire clippers for trimming line knots, elastic bands for securing floats to line etc. An army camouflaged baseball cap or 'brimmed' hat to keep the sun out of your eyes. 'Ready made' dead bait rigs. A medium - large 'water-proof' heavy duty, back pack - preferably army camouflaged or plain or neutral coloured like green, black, grey or brown. A couple of slices of white bread or a small tub of worms or maggots for catching bait. A good quality, strong, large 'mouthed' long handled landing net. An accurate pair of weighing scales - preferably electronic or digital scales but if not then luggage/baggage scales. A large unhooking mat. A good strong leather belt for attaching 'looped' wire traces, car keys (to the metal buckle) and two pouches for my multi (unhooking) tools. A mobile phone for emergencies. A mobile phone or camera for photographing large fish. Chocolate/candy bars, snacks, bananas, water/energy drinks.

In winter: Fingerless gloves, a deer stalker hat or suitable thick, warm, wooly hat, thick socks, a warm jacket/coat or 'body warmer.'

This list is not exhaustive, it is just designed to give you a rough idea of what you will need for your next pike fishing expedition. I have 3 'ready made' set ups - one for lure fishing, one for live/deadbaiting and one for nightfishing. I suggest that you do the same... They all have various things in common but they are all 'slightly' different.

CHAPTER 6.
LOCATING 'BIG' PIKE

INTO ANOTHER WORLD... (The lair of the pike)

I lay in my lair, pretending to sleep...
Each moment aware, of every movement and creep.
My eyes are open, my senses keen
To each flicker of silver amidst the green.
I feel each vibration, I taste every smell...
I'm as hungry as a lion but no one else can tell
As I lay in the darkness, preparing to strike -
Whoever be foolish and stray from the light...

I'm the king of the jungle - let there be no doubt
And I prey on roach and perch and trout
My fins are powerful, my teeth are sharp
And I prey on tench and bream and carp.
Frogs and newts and toads beware!
I'll eat them all and none I'll spare!
I'm as fast as lightning, I'm as cold as ice
I'm as greedy as a glutton and I never think twice!

I know the water rat and the vole...
Every entrance and every exit, to every tunnel and every hole.
I know the frogs and the season they spawn
And I've watched the duckling from the day he was born.
I know where the shoals swim and the lay of the fry
And I view them all - through a ruthless hunters eyes
I will suffer no rivals - whoever they may be

And I will show no pity, for mercy deserts me

I know the moorhen and the coot
I spy out their nests and follow their routes,
The greedy fat perch and the solitary trout
I see them and feel them and sniff them all out,
The minnow, the stickleback and the gudgeon too
I show no preference - any easy snack will do.
I'm aware of the heron, and the fishermen too
I slip into deep water. There's nothing they can do...

The slimy eel and the greedy young jack
If they stray too close, I'm sure to attack
The gosling, the mallard and the fat, feathered duck
If they come too close, they'll run out of luck.
I know the bullhead and the fat wart backed toad
I catch them and eat them by the bucket load
The frogs and birds that live on these lakes
I even eat newts, lizards and snakes!

I hope you enjoyed that little rhyme. I wrote it purely for illustrative purposes of course...

If you are not catching any pike/fish... This is usually because of one of several reasons. Here are 3 of them...

1. You are fishing in the wrong place... The wrong location, swim, peg, stretch of river/canal etc. Wrong place, wrong time/ time of day.

2. Fishing competition/pressure... Somebody else has 'hit that spot' the day/week before you and beat you to it and probably had a cracking days fishing (at your expense.)

3. Ultimately, you have to remember that pike (and predators) are more than capable of catching their own food! They are after all - super efficient hunters. They really don't need our 'charity

offerings' to survive. Seriously, they don't need our leftover deadbaits. They do pretty well all on their own. Especially in food dense/rich fisheries. In 'hard to fish' places like this (and I have fished some of them) there is too much 'natural' food (competition) for your hook bait/lure. Sometimes you are better off just fishing somewhere else where there is less fishing 'pressure' and less competition!

Locating 'BIG' pike can be the difficult part...

To give you an idea of how difficult this can be, let me tell you a short story...

WILY OLD PIKE...

I know of a fisherman who whilst fishing on a large lake saw a huge, monster pike. He told me that whilst reeling in his line he noticed what he thought was a huge log in the water near the bank where he was fishing. His attention was drawn to it when the 'log' started moving in front of him! He said that he was so shocked when he realised that the log was in fact a pike that his first initial reaction was to take a step backwards away from it! My initial reaction would have been the opposite, I would have taken a step closer towards it and probably rugby tackled it crocodile hunter style! Now, this man has told me that his personal best pike is twenty six pounds! So you would think that it would take a considerable amount to shock him but shocked he was! I have very good reason to believe his story is true as you will soon see...

CROCODILE HUNTING!

He told all his friends and fellow fishermen about it and the next time I saw him there were about eight or ten lads fishing from a peg about the size of a double decker bus - all with livebaits out!

The following evening there were another five or six lads all fishing in that same spot. I bumped into one of the lads outside a shop and asked him if any of them had caught the 'monster' pike yet? "No" he said, "and four or five of us went back every night for a week and fished with livebaits but we never caught him." "Hmm" I said, "interesting." After this I bumped into the man who had originally told me the story. "No, we never caught it" he said, "and I was surprised, because pike are territorial aren't they?" he said. I thought to myself... "They are territorial alright, the problem is that the pike sees the whole lake (all his environment) as HIS TERRITORY."

HAPPY HUNTING GROUND

The pike is already in his very own "happy hunting ground."

Allow me to explain... Pike are nomadic. Nomadic means that they are constantly on the move, prowling around, on the hunt, swimming around, moving from place to place, from position to position, patrolling the waterways, playing a high risk, winner takes all game of cat and mouse with the prey/shoal fish, waterfowl, water voles, rats etc. Constantly following, creeping, moving, swimming, chasing, being chased, stalking and hunting. With intervals where they lie in wait to ambush something or rest up to digest their last meal. They are like pieces on a chess board constantly looking for a better, 'superior' position from which to hunt their prey!

WHERE THE PREY ARE...THERE THE PIKE ARE...

A CONSTANTLY CHANGING ENVIRONMENT

Remember this: No matter how well you 'think' you know a piece of water - the fish know it better than you do and what you see from the bank or the surface of the water might be nothing like a true reflection of the secret underwater realm of pike and predators.

Just because you caught a particular pike or fish in a particular place does not mean that they are bound to be there again and magically reappear on demand.

Sometimes a big fish is caught in a certain place and never seen again, or not seen again for a long time, sometimes a very long time. What was a pleasurable experience for you (catching the fish) was undoubtably not a pleasurable experience for the fish. You will both remember the experience but for completely different reasons. Yes, pike are territorial but they are also freespirited, restless, nomadic creatures. They roam around from day to day and hour to hour. If the pike were always hiding or lurking in the exact same place then the shoal of prey fish would have a very easy time avoiding them. The reality is that the pike is a very efficient predator - an extremely efficient predator. He is constantly reacting or responding to his environment or environmental changes around him. Seasonal changes, weather changes, variations in water depth, water clarity or dis-colouration, weed/plant growth or decline, danger in the form of other predators, prey behaviour and food availability. If pike (and other predators) did not constantly adapt to their environment then they would not be the incredibly adept and successful predators that they are and in some places they would have been wiped out long before now.

THIS IS ONE OF THE WONDERS AND MYSTERIES OF PIKE FISHING...

<u>DO PIKE BECOME 'WISE'?</u>

Having kept pike in tanks for nearly 15 years I can assure you that they do in fact learn very fast... From the youngest age they are constantly learning and adapting to their environment. They are also a very curious, inquisitive fish. My pike have taken just as much of an interest in me as I have in them. I am fascinated by their feeding habits and surprisingly - they are fascinated by mine! Whenever I eat in front of them they seem to take a keen interest in what I am doing or more specifically - what I am eating! They learn very quickly that when I open the fish tank lid - food is coming, usually in the form of a big fat juicy worm! **Where a lot of anglers go wrong is that they do not understand that a big pike is a truly wild fish.** They should be treat with the same amount of respect as a big carp. Everyone knows that carp get wise. So do big pike.

I have no doubt that pike do have the ability to become 'wise' as they get bigger and older. When they have come under heavy pressure from anglers, they sometimes, still manage to avoid or evade capture (sometimes for years.) Even when the angling press have exposed them and made them famous, and every angler in the country knows their whereabouts, and still, despite the best efforts of the so called 'elite' fishermen they remain uncaught.

Who knows if a pike learns to associate a fishermans presence on the bank with danger, or a boat, or a fishing rod, or a pike float, or a particular type of lure that they have been caught on previously, or even a particular colour, or even the peg, or area where they were last caught! We simply do not know exactly how a pike's mind or 'brain' works.

Consider this: What is a pike's/fish's or any other living creatures number one perogative, goal or overriding instinct? The answer is simple, the answer is to SURVIVE. Survival is the first law of nature. Only the strong survive. Survival of the fittest is the expression, or in this case - the wisest.

A hungry pike is easier to catch than a full pike but a starving pike is even easier to catch still, In theory. I put it to you that big pike do indeed become 'wise' with the passage of time, or at least wiser than their smaller and younger brethren - the over eager jacks which 'hang' themselves on a daily basis. A pike's overriding survival instinct tells it that it has to - nay must - hunt and eat in order to survive. It really is a jungle out there!

NO SUBSTITUTE FOR EXPERIENCE

I have fished some 'hard' waters where big pike practically NEVER touch lures. The jacks up to four or five pounds will chase and hit them all day long, but the bigger pike will only take live and deadbaits. No doubt, these fish have probably been caught on a spinner, spoon, lure or plug back in the day, when they were young jacks. Perhaps once or twice or maybe even half a dozen times or more. But somewhere along the passage of time they became 'wise' or 'mature' and ceased to bother responding to, chasing, or hitting lures. My guess is that this all relates to fishing pressure, lure 'traffic' and other factors. Trying to tempt or catch a big pike in a water that has an over or 'super' abundance of natural prey fish can be very difficult for any fisherman. The pike is more than capable of catching his own supper...

You may have guessed that I am speaking from experience. I have fished some very 'hard' waters. You have got to remember: The really big pike in Scottish lochs and Irish lakes rarely ever see a lure unless they catch it! The lure 'traffic' is almost non-existent. Lures are few and far between in those places. So they can be caught on big lures - on a right time, right place basis.

LOCATION, LOCATION, LOCATION

Just because you saw a big pike down by the fallen tree on monday morning does not guarantee that she will be there on monday evening... She may be... Or she may be down by the old wooden bridge, or she may have moved underneath the old willow tree. She may be down by the big rocks or she may have swam out into deep water between the islands! She might be sat on the edge of one of the islands, watching a nest, with her eye on a baby coot chick! She may have followed that coot family half way across the lake, waiting for her moment to strike. She could be down by the muddy banks hiding in the bushy undergrowth digesting a coot chick whilst simultaneously waiting for a water vole to come out of his hole.

She could be lying underneath a collapsed bank digesting a big rat! She could be lying in the shallows, on some gravel, basking in the sun, trying to warm up a bit! She could by lying on top of an underwater spring trying to stay cool. She may be facing the in flow of a small river or stream to regulate her rising body temperature whilst simultaneously keeping her eye out for fish. She could be cruising out in open water chasing a shoal of roach, perch, chub or carp. She may be laid up resting under the lilly pads, digesting last nights carp supper. She may have moved underneath a big piece of weed to lie in wait for her next meal. She may be watching a coot or moorhen near some bull rushes. she may be back underneath the fallen tree digesting a big belly full of eel or lamprey!

It gets complicated, doesn't it? I have laboured my point a bit here but you get my message - to a big pike - everywhere is <u>HIS</u> territory! It's a bit like a human being, you live in a house but you travel around everywhere, in your local town, city, or even further afield.

SHROUDED IN MYSTERY

A truly big pike's life, habits, movements and whereabouts may be completely shrouded in mystery...

The point that I am trying to make is that the pike is the king of his own jungle, and there is nowhere on a big piece of water that he will not have explored or have become very familiar, and intimate with, at some point in his travels. He will explore every square inch of his habitat and environment, which will also be constantly changing with the weather and the seasons.

Read my poem/s (about pike) I did not write them purely for entertainment purposes only - there are lessons in them...

UNSEEN AND UNKNOWN MONSTERS

I have no doubts whatsoever, that all throughout history, many wily, old, record, or trophy pike have probably lay down on the bottom of deep lakes and rivers and died of old age, disease, or natural causes without anyone ever knowing anything about it, or ever being seen or caught by anyone in their lifetime. At least not seen out of the water, or on the bank by anyone. Especially in Irish loughs, Scottish lochs, the Norfolk Broads and places like that. If these pike ever were caught it would have been in their youth (when they were jacks) or only ever once or twice in their entire lifetime and most likely not at their peak weight.

Maybe, they have been hooked once or twice but never landed...

TERRITORIAL PIKE

Pike ARE territorial. If the best place to hunt is underneath the lily pads or near the bullrushes then you can bet your bottom dollar that the pike will be there... However, in a constantly changing environment which is what many rivers, ponds, and lakes are. The pike have to go with the flow and follow the available food sources or prey items. If insects hatch in a particular location then you can guarantee that the coarse fish will know about it and capitalise on it. The fish will go where the most readily available food sources are. The pike go where the prey go. Sometimes on a big piece of water, where food or prey items are not so readily available, a pike may have to travel a lot to hunt and survive. A pike may swim several miles up and down a river or canal. A pike may cover acres of water in a big lake. Me and my fishing buddy have both caught the same two fish once each on one of our local lakes. We both caught them in completely different places though - on opposite sides of the same lake and in two different pegs. I rest my case. Pike are nomadic. In fact, all fish are - except those trapped in a goldfish bowl, and given the option, I'm sure they would like to have a wander as well. Pike are territorial but a pike may have a dozen or even fifty hidey holes or ambush points or whatever you want to call them on a big lake, pond, river or canal. Sometimes many pike have to share the same ambush points and each one may be constantly occupied by a different pike at different times, on different days - after all - they are all competing for the same food sources. Now and then, a big one bumps into a little one and that is usually when two become one!

<u>HOTSPOTS</u>

There are 'hotspots' where you tend to find lots of pike in one place and you cannot always tell why a place is a hotspot even though you know that it is.

I have a theory on why you sometimes catch several pike in the same spot. Sometimes it's because that is the best hunting spot, geographically speaking. Where all the shoal fish or prey fish are congregated together and all the pike are lured to the same spot by a shared common interest - they're hungry!

Me and a group of friends once spent all day fishing with lures for pike with no luck. At about 7pm we had all had enough and all but given up. Somebody made one last cast and hooked a pike in an un-fished peg so we all carried on fishing with renewed interest. We then caught a total of about 7 pike in the space of about half an hour. it seemed that all the pike had the same idea and were all holed up in the same swim in a narrow channel that ran parallel with an island on the water. They were lying in wait in the path of the unsuspecting carp and shoal fish that used this channel. Sometimes it is just a case of luck and being in the right place at the right time...

THE PIKE IS A TRULY WILD AND MYSTERIOUS FISH in the purest, rawest sense.

Locating big pike is easier said than done. The hardest part of pike fishing and catching big pike is often finding them. They can be anywhere and nowhere all at the same time and it can be very time consuming and frustrating to say the least. To say that pike live in rivers, canals, ponds, lakes, lochs and loughs is nothing more than hot air and stating the obvious. When you are fishing a huge expanse of water that is hundreds of feet deep, miles long, covers acres or represents literally tons of water - the crucial question remains...

WHERE ARE THE FISH?

That is a question that I cannot answer for you. You have to do the leg work, groundwork, homework, study and research for yourself.

I can however, give you a few pointers: Big pike like deep water. However, when they are cold they like to bask in the sun in shallower water. They like features and overhead structures that represent safety and security from other predators such as birds of prey and man who is seen as yet another predator or threat to the pike's survival.

They like ambush points and hidey holes. They like to live near islands, out in the middle of lakes or ponds - in deep inaccessible places far away from man. They like hiding beneath undercut banks. They like complicated (twisting) 'tree root' patterns and overhanging trees such as willow trees. They like to live near or beneath wooden, metal or concrete bridges, fallen trees, or logs. They like overhanging bushes, they like places that are destitute, overgrown, rural, wild, or quiet (like nature reserves.) They like places that are overgrown or inaccessible to man such as very deep water, out in the middle of huge lakes. They like to cruise through the middle of channels in between islands on big lakes. They like the shade of lilly pads in summer and reeds or reed stems in winter. They like to lie beneath surface weed and amongst underwater weed. Where there is surface weed and underwater weed there are pike. They can be found near and among bull rushes (they spawn there.)

They like to hide in the shade and the shadows beneath boats on canals, in marinas or boat docking yards. Like 'vampires' They do not like direct sunlight as it exposes them. They like to remain highly camouflaged, unseen, undetected, and invisible or imperceptible. On small rivers we used to always find/catch them beneath the green surface weed or 'scum' that builds up on the surface in the summer months. Just drop your bait on the edge and hold on tight...

Where there are small, shoal fish or prey fish - there are pike. Where there are pike - there are 'other' pike. What I mean is this: Pike being cannibals are both predator and prey for other pike. Where you see or catch one pike - you are more than likely to encounter other pike in the near vicinity. Where there are small birds or waterfowl - there are pike. Where there are frogs there are pike...

THE SECRET IS TO LOCATE THE PIKE'S FOOD SOURCE. IF YOU CAN FIND THE PIKE'S FOOD SOURCE THEN YOU CAN FIND THE PIKE...

The other way to do it is to find the place where the pike feel most at home... Comfortable, safe, secure or protected.

But be aware that a fish's location will change as his preferred food source changes and this is usually dependent on the four seasons and their unique feeding opportunities.

THE HUNTER IS NEVER FOUND FAR FROM HIS QUARRY...

Be that a shoal of fish swimming through their favourite swim, some young fry hiding in the shallows, fish spawning, A waterbird's nest, young chicks swimming with their mother or fat frogs full of spawn and ready to burst...

FROGS, TOADS AND PIKE

Where there are frogs or toads breeding/spawning there are pike...

I once walked about 3 miles down a canal in pursuit of big pike in clear water. I could not find them. I could only see small jacks! I walked back to the beginning and turned right and headed upstream instead. Within 5 minutes I had found several big, fat, well nourished pike all laying about on the bottom of the canal in close proximity to each other. They were at least double figures and some of them possibly twenty pounds or more in weight.

There was not a jack or a prey fish to be seen anywhere, not even a stickleback. What has attracted them to this spot I wondered? I immediately noted that the water was 5 or 6 feet deep in places but I knew that, that was not the answer as I had seen other likely looking deep swims downstream of this point with no fish in them. Then I looked on the bottom of the canal and saw dozens of fat frogs all on top of each other pairing up and breeding! That was the answer!

The big pike were all lazing about doing nothing. I was pretty sure that they had been stuffing themselves full of fat frogs, gorging themselves and then laying about to digest their heavy meal. Knowing full well that there was plenty more where they came from. The frogs being completely distracted and fully focussed on reproducing, this made them very easy prey and gave the pike the freedom to feed at their own leisure, without a care in the world and without the need to go actively hunting in pursuit of food. Rich pickings, easy pickings and all right on their doorstep!

A SEASONAL FISH

Nature has her seasons and it is my firm belief that all creatures and especially fish are very conscious and aware of the different seasons and their unique feeding opportunities. In the same way that a farmer knows what crops grow and harvest in each season. An ordinary person like you or I might come to expect to pick blackberries for blackberry pie or crumble in august or september.

Take for example: The trout expecting and eating the mayflies in may.

The pike know through instinct, or past experience when the

frogs breed or spawn. When fish are laden with eggs, when chicks are born, ducklings, coots and so on.

That is how they are able to feed themselves throughout the four seasons of the year - spring, summer, autumn and winter.

Like us, they learn from past experiences, they remember previous years, and they come to expect, and even rely and depend on various different food sources - seasonally.

FROGGY STYLE

One time when I was fishing another pond I noticed that the frogs were breeding on the bottom of the pond. I had a frog imitation lure on at the time. An incredibly unrealistic brown one I might add. So having a sense of humour (and a mischievious nature) I thought that I would drop it in amongst the breeding frogs and see what they made of it! (I know, I know) Imagine my surprise when the frogs all started making a beeline for my fake rubber frog! Incredible, I thought, they must be desperate!

FROG LURE FRENZY

Another time I was fishing a short stretch of wild, overgrown canal on a deep bend. I do not know exactly how deep the water is on this stretch (I wouldn't like to fall in put it that way) but I would say six feet deep at the very least as the water is very dark and you cannot see the bottom.

I cast out a rubber frog imitation lure towards the opposite bank and began to work it along the surface slowly... hop, hop, hop...

All of a sudden a pike burst out of the deep water straight up in a vertical line and struck at my lure. He missed and fell back into the water. Amazingly, he immediately shot straight back up at my lure. Missing again by the narrowest of margins. Incredibly this same pike did the same thing several times before hitting my frog lure. His head just kept bursting out of the water in a vertical line. This was something that I had never seen a pike do before - a vertical strike, numerous times in rapid succession! I caught said pike and upon examination noticed that it was blind in one eye! This may go someway towards explaining why he was so over eager, and kept just missing the mark.

Another time I was walking around a lake and noticed some lily pads to my right. I dropped in a rubber frog lure, in 2 feet of water, at a rods length, at the edge of the lily pads. Immediately a long, streamlined pike shot right out in front of me with super aggression and confidence and took my frog at once without a moments hesitation. I caught that pike as well, and without even having to cast out!

TRY RUBBER FROG LURES - THEY WORK AND SOMETIMES THEY INDUCE 'UBER' AGGRESSIVE SUPER CONFIDENT TAKES!

In order to find the pike it helps to understand them. What are their needs, motives, priorities. Their main needs are food and 'shelter' or (safety/security.)

Their main motive is to hide from other predators and hunt prey. Their priorities are two and joint... **hiding** from other predators and **hunting** prey or feeding and staying safe

1. lying in wait, hiding in ambush to surprise, attack, capture and eat prey fish and any other prey creatures, mammals, birds or animals.

and

2. Hiding from other predators and staying safe, alive and surviving.

FOR THE PIKE: STEALTH = SURVIVAL

A pike's life is like a big game of high stakes, winner takes all hide and seek. Hide and hunt. hunt and hide. This is a pike's life. A pike is like a fugitive on the run from the police. Constantly lying low and being stealthy, sneaky, quick and discrete - discretion is the name of the game.

GATHERING INTELLIGENCE

Look on the internet, study photographs of previously caught fish, enquire at the local tackle shop, ask the locals, do whatever it takes, but gather intelligence you must.

Expect to be told a few 'porky pies' (lies) and deliberately misled by your fellow anglers and rival fishermen as this is all part of the game. You have to trust your instincts and learn to seperate the wheat from the chaff. I have to admit it bugs me when I catch a big pike or any big fish for that matter and the first thing that flies out of a fellow (rival) anglers mouth is: "Where did you catch that then?" Usually followed by "what did you catch it on?" And sometimes "I'm after that big one that you caught!" I'm guilty of asking the same questions myself, but hey it's all part of the game. I have my secrets but hey - I've been on a few wild goose trails myself! If you are going to tell everyone (everything you catch) all of the time, then you might as well give up fishing! Don't tell your local tackle dealer everything you catch and where you caught it as he is in the tackle trade... It is in his best interests to tell anyone and everyone who walks into his shop about every noteworthy fish that has been caught recently as this improves sales of fishing tackle! It's a business after all and these guys know all the tricks!

LEARN HOW TO KEEP A SECRET...

With the passage of time, I have learned how to be crafty and wily (like an old farmer) when it comes to big fish, and I suggest that you do the same...

I always try to be as open and honest as I can with people, but when it comes to a big fish I can be very guarded. Sometimes, you have to be... I call it "looking out for your own best interests" or 'protecting your investments.'

ALWAYS TRUST YOUR NATURAL INSTINCTS...

When deciding where to fish such as which stretches of river/ canal or which pegs on a large pond or lake. Go with your gut...

Never be afraid to try something completely different or out of the ordinary...

Such as a new fishing spot, stretch of river or canal, natural or artificial bait, homemade or modified lure, method or technique. It might just pay off.

CHAPTER 7. CONSULTING THE EXPERTS...

<u>THE BIRD EATING MONSTER</u>

Back in late June 2013, I was working my way around a large lake in a strategic, methodical fashion (as per usual.) When I came to a particular peg, which although it looked very promising had not been producing the goods as of late. I decided to skip this peg and move on to the next peg in search of greener pastures. I fished the next peg for a fruitless half an hour or so before deciding to head back.

On the way back I changed my mind and decided to have a crack at the last peg (the one I skipped) after all. What happened next had never happened to me before this time and I have experienced it just once since. That's twice in over thirty years of fishing!

Night was falling... I made my way through some bushes to a peg that was nicely situated smack bang in the middle of two islands. I put my back pack down and momentarily turned my back on the water for the briefest of moments. I took off my lure and switched it to a luminous green Rapala surface lure with a small propeller blade on the back. (Designed to imitate a small wounded fish struggling along on the surface of the water.)

The lake that I was fishing is a natural fishery that is fed by a river and very popular with all manner of wild birds - swans, geese, ducks, moorhens, coots, divers, herons and lots of other birds. I had my back to the water, had just placed my rucksack down on the ground and was in the process of attaching a new lure to my wire leader...

All of a sudden I heard the tell tale swooshing sound of a flying bird - landing on the surface of the lake. This sound is quite the norm and nothing out of the ordinary, so I thought nothing of it, until I heard the sound of the same bird squawking and flapping its wings about as it struggled to stay above the surface of the water. I span around in an instant to face the bird and see what was distressing it. Just as I looked at the bird - it went under the water. Due to me facing the wrong way and the near dark conditions I could not get a positive id on the bird - Unfortunately. Not being a bird expert, I could not tell what species of bird it was, based on the 'squawking' sounds it made before being dragged under the water. I strained my eyes in focus and concentration to see what happened next and to see if the bird came back up to the surface of the water... It didn't.

Instead, I saw a large 'bow wave' and the silhouette of a fish swimming away (in deep water) towards the near bank, into a 'cove' behind a bush which I must presume is the pike's/fish's 'lair'. I can only deduce from what I saw and heard that a medium (moorhen/coot to duck) sized bird made the mistake of doing a waterski type landing manoeuvre on the surface of the lake after nightfall and inadvertently slowed down and came to an abrupt stop right in front of a large, hungry, hunting, female pike's nose! Whether that pike was there by chance or by design I cannot be sure but what I witnessed got me thinking...

Perhaps this is not such an isolated incident after all... Could it be that big, hungry, female pike deliberately wait until nightfall to hunt and ambush wild birds on the surface of the water, which give themselves away by their loud splashing and noisy landings? After all, why would a big pike go to the trouble of hunting all day to catch a roach or a perch when she can just wait until nightfall when she is almost invisible and imperceptible. Then silently, stealthily approach a bird from beneath the water or pick off stray birds at will, as and when the mood strikes.

It could be that this happens all the time, during the night, under the cover of darkness, when no - one is around to witness it. After all, there aren't that many people (like me) who would be willing to hang around in spooky places like this, at night, Just for the sake of catching a big fish! I checked the time on my watch that the pike had taken the bird. It was around 10.20pm. Strange, right around the same time that I had caught a big pike on a Salmo (half pound) carp imitation lure on a peg nearby.

Coincidence? who knows. Could it be the exact same fish? or could it be that all the big pike in this water come on the feed at around about the same time? Could it be that the really big predators are nightfeeders? That would explain why they are so hard to catch during the day. Have they turned 'nightfeeder' due to fishing pressure? Or have they turned bird eater due to there being a super abundance of wild birds living on and around these waters?

Was it truly a monster pike? Or could it have been a big catfish? To my knowledge - there are no catfish in these waters - not naturally at least. Only rumours of catfish... but enough rumours to get me wondering... Could somebody have released a catfish or more than one catfish into this lake? I personally have never seen or caught one... but that doesn't mean that they are not here. Something had to account for that bird, something big, that hunts at night...

Over ten years later... An old friend of mine who has fished this water all his life told me that he had seen a big Catfish in the lake... That it had "swam right past him." I have no cause to doubt him. Perhaps somebody introduced the Wels Catfish into this lake many years ago without telling anybody else about it... Perhaps there's more than one, that would explain what I witnessed that night.

THE BIRD EATING MONSTER - PART TWO

I mentioned witnessing this type of occurrence twice... The second time I was watching two adult coots (small black water birds with a little white patch on their noses.) They had 3 baby coots with them and they were swimming around near a distant island (coincidently, a friend of mine had recently caught a double figure pike in the exact same area.)

All of a sudden I heard splashing and a commotion near the island where the coots and coot chicks were swimming. I looked up but thought nothing of it at first. I thought it was just birds fighting or squabbling (a very common occurrence.) Then I noticed a bow-wave and a trail of bubbles coming up to the surface...

Strange! I thought to myself. The trail of bubbles went around the island, across the lake and along the bank of another island, before disappearing into deep water in the middle of two islands. I know, because I followed the bubbles for as long as I could in hopes of catching sight of the culprit.

I never did see the fish properly. It was too far away and swimming away too quickly out into deep water. I looked back at the coots. There were now two adults and two chicks. Whatever it was (most probably a pike) had taken one of the baby coot chicks and all it took was a precious second and there was very little that the parents could do to protect their young.

Since then I have not seen any coot chicks on the lake. Surprise, surprise, but I have managed to catch three or four jacks on a small, homemade, black lure that looks like and imitates a coot chick! Well, you can't blame me for trying can you?

I believe small birds such as coot chicks, moorhen chicks, baby ducklings, divers and even goslings (baby geese) all fall victim to pike predation every year and alot more often than we realise. We simply don't see it because we are not looking for it and sometimes it happens at night under the cover of darkness or at first or last light when nobody is around to see it.

TWO BIG PIKE AND A DEAD RAT!

I never forgot what happened on that peg on that dark spooky night. I told my fishing buddy about it and knowing me like he does he had no doubts about the truth of my account. The bird eating pike fired up our imaginations and we soon set off to catch the greedy culprit...

We were careful not to tell anybody exactly where it had happened for fear that they might catch the "bird eating monster" before we had a chance to get our hooks into him.

We sneaked down the overgrown, winding path that led to the weedy peg between two islands in the middle of a large lake. My fishing buddy fired out a small perch on a pike float... It landed in the exact spot where the bird was eaten. The float went under and disappeared! It had been taken - instantly! Me and my buddy both looked at each other at the same time - we couldn't believe it! I hoped it was 'the big one' that took the bird.

My friend wound his line down tight and did his trademark strike. He connected, the fish was on. He played the fish in slowly with a big smile plastered all over his face. His rod was fully bent into the fish which was taking off on spectacular runs and stripping line off the reel. From a distance it did not look like a huge fish but as it got closer to the bank, it got bigger and bigger.

I only had a small landing net on me so I had to land the fish by hand. No problem, I chinned the pike, we unhooked it and quickly noticed that it had a big lump in its throat/chest area which was obviously it's last meal.

I opened its mouth and did my trademark trick of looking down its throat to examine its last meal. There was a tail hanging out of the back of the pikes throat... Only this wasn't a fish's tail... This was a rat's tail!! And a rather big rat judging on the size of the tail, the size of the pike, and the size of the big bulge in the pike's belly! It must have been a big rat to have been swallowed by a pike that size and still have 5 inches of tail on show! Urghh - gross!

We put it back - and quickly. Handling fish is one thing, I don't mind that, I'm used to that. Handling rats is another. No thank you, you can keep it! Yuk, but still, did that big female take that rat off the surface of the water under cover of darkness? Did she know it was a rat or did she think it was something else?

I have seen something like this once before: I caught a pike on a surface popper. When I looked down his throat I noticed some brown fur and a tail hanging out. I took this to be a water vole at the time but I suppose thinking about it now, it could have been a rat... (Watervoles only live on average 5 months) quite possibly due to predation. They are quite simply 'easy meat!'

Another time, I deliberately fashioned a homemade lure to look like a rat as there were a lot of rats or water voles living in the immediate vicinity around the banks of the particular stretch of river that I was fishing. I cast out downstream off of a wooden bridge that I was standing on. As I was reeling in my line with 'rat' lure swimming upstream along the surface, a pike of about 3 feet long and at least 10 pounds or so shot out from under the bank and gave chase to my lure at high speed. At the last second, he saw me standing on the wooden bridge, turned back from my lure and swam back into his hiding place under the weeds.

My brother bought a mouse/rat imitation lure on holiday and informed me that he caught nearly a dozen pike on that lure before he retired it in a tree! That is why surface/topwater lures are so effective and successful - because pike take a lot of their prey off the surface of the water, after all - a rat's gotta drink too!

Small rivers are sometimes full of rat holes, rats and water voles and I can't help but believe based on my own experiences and observations that a pike's diet consists of a lot more rats, water voles, frogs, toads and small mammals than a lot of anglers and lure manufacturers could possibly ever realise. After all a pike is by nature a largely opportunistic hunter or predator. So remember my words... The next time you catch a nice pike and you are thinking about taking it home for the pot. Otherwise you might get a nasty surprise when you slit that belly - Yuck! Think of all them diseases... Rather you than me! Just remember you heard it here first! As I mentioned... The average water vole's life expectancy is only 5 months! I wonder if the pike have anything to do with that?

BACK TO THE STORY...

My friend cast out another small perch into a spot almost identical to the first cast and we waited... After about 20 minutes to half an hour - the float went down and started making off in the opposite direction again! My friend struck and was quickly into another big pike and loving every second of it. Two big pike in the same swim? A big smile plastered all over his face as he heaved into the fish, rod bent double and reel clutch letting off line as the big pike went on run after run. Eventually the pike tired out and he reeled her in. I hand landed the pike for him and much to our surprise she was even bigger than the first pike! I looked down her throat but it seemed that she hadn't eaten anything substantial that day.

DISTRESS SIGNALS

Sometimes the splashing and struggling of a hooked pike fighting on rod and line can arouse the interest or curiosity of a pike of a similiar or bigger size and draw him or her in from further up or downstream, or from the next peg, or even quite a considerable distance away - the struggle excites him. That is why fishermen often get their fish grabbed or seized by pike and why pike often grab other pike, for the same reason that they cannot resist a livebait offering - because another fish in distress attracts or interests them and arouses or triggers their predatory instinct and often results in an imminent, aggressive attack.

Pike and catfish know how to home in on a nice easy meal. Ever heard the expression "a sitting duck?" If you are planning on livebaiting, deadbaiting or even lure fishing a big piece of water and you are wondering how to locate pike or even catfish, sometimes it is worth bearing in mind that hungry, opportunistic pike (and catfish) won't be too far away from waterfowl and especially their young or nests.

<u>PIKE AND WATERFOWL</u>

I once spoke to a wildlife expert who has been working with, and observing water birds/fowl for many years. He listed some of the birds that pike like to eat (this is based on his own observations and experience over the years.)

He has never physically seen a pike take or eat a bird... I have (in real life) it was a baby coot. He simply releases birds (sometimes rare birds) into the wild and then observes them with his binoculars, and catalogues, or keeps tabs on their numbers, updating his records on a daily basis...

According to the 'expert' pike eat many types of waterfowl or birds...

Ducks, mallards and more commonly baby ducklings. Moorhens and their young, coots and their young. Young, immature herons. Divers and their young (which cannot dive until they are mature.) As well as other birds.

He informed me that he once released 10 rare white ducks into the wild and came back to observe them on a daily basis... It went something like this... Day 1 there were 10. Day 2 there were 7 or 8. Day 3 there were 4 or 5. Day 4 there were 2 or 3. Day 5 there was 1. Day 6 there were none. Something along those lines. He told me that there is one particular species of water bird which he has never seen survive to maturity in the wild in the last 16 years...

Again he puts this down to pike eating them. He says that the water authorities once discussed electro-netting some of the waters and killing the pike but were unable to do so due to the water being too deep. The water has to be four or five feet deep but these lakes are twelve or more feet deep in places.

In defence of the pike there were lots of swans, geese and adult ducks and mallards on these pieces of water as well as numerous medium and small sized birds like coots and moorhens.

I have also seen a carp eat a baby duckling (on youtube) so you cannot lay all the blame on the pike as there are numerous and very large carp on these waters as well, who could also potentially be the guilty culprits.

Also, if there are any catfish in any of these waters they are well known to predate on birds at any opportunity - even pigeons!

PIKE, GEESE AND GOSLING CHICKS

One day I took a walk around said lake with my friend. We noticed two adult geese swimming with three young goslings. I said to my friend "there should be a lot more than three chicks in tow, you know?" "Do you reckon?" he said. "Yes" I replied. "Keep your eye out for any more geese swimming with their young..." We carried on walking around the lake. There were many geese everywhere but at last we came upon two sets of geese and gosling (young geese) The first family was a family of eight - two adults and six young. The second family was a family of fifteen! Two adults and thirteen young 'baby' goslings. I turned and said to my friend "look, that family of eight has two adults and six (larger, more mature gosling) but that other family of fifteen has two adults and thirteen (small, young) chicks. My guess is that if all of these families started out with thirteen chicks each, then the first family we saw lost ten chicks due to predation and the second family lost seven chicks. That's seventeen gosling or geese chicks lost in only a matter of weeks! My guess is that this is a conservative estimate and that even the family with thirteen chicks may have already lost some chicks due to predatory pike activity on this lake. That tells me that there is a very healthy population of pike living on these waters. My guess is that a five pound (or so) pike can easily take a baby gosling. I would also go so far as to say that the pike come to expect, even rely upon the birth of young waterfowl and eating them every year in order to guarantee their own survival. The fact remains that the youngest family had the most chicks (thirteen) the next oldest family had larger and less (six) chicks in total. Of the oldest and more mature family only three large goslings remained. Now, I am not a bird expert by any means but these are my observations and the conclusions which I have drawn from them. Young gosling are after all EASY PREY and pike are greedy, opportunistic predators. What do you expect? Nature is just doing its thing...

CHAPTER 8. IN DEFENCE OF THE PIKE

THE PIKE'S ROLE IN NATURE

Part of the pike's job or place in the ecosystem is disease control. By eating dying, diseased and dead fish, the pike helps to stop the spread of disease in our waters. He does in fact, serve a purpose in nature. The bigger a pike becomes, the more partial he is to scavenging dead fish off of the bottom. That is why so many big pike are caught using dead sea fish for bait. Even though a pike may never have seen these species of (sea) fish before. It is his rightful duty and obligation to eat them. Number 1. To prevent the potential spread of disease and 2. To ensure his own survival.

The really big pike - twenties, thirties and forty pounders probably exist on a diet of mainly diseased, dying and dead fish scavenged off of the bottom. Whatever dies, is quickly eaten and therefore placed back into the ecosystem or food chain. This is the circle of life.

In nature there are no dustbins or landfill sites, *nothing* is wasted. This ensures the balance of nature and a clean healthy living environment for the fish living in our waters.

Any one who has ever kept fish in a fish tank or aquarium or worked in a pet store will be able to tell you: When a fish dies, it becomes harmful or detrimental to the health of the remaining fish living in that environment to leave the dead fish in the water. If the dead fish is not 'eaten' or removed from the water within a short time of dying it could cause the death of all the other fish in that water.

Hopefully this goes some way towards explaining the pike's job or role in the ecosystem as 'waste disposal unit' and helps the ignorant to understand that the pike are here for a reason, they are 'meant' to be in our waters. And they serve a very important purpose: That of disposing of dying, diseased and dead fish and preventing the spread of disease in our waters. The presence of pike in our waters, is not a bad thing, it is a very good thing and helps to ensure that our waters remain healthy and free of disease.

It is about time that people (especially anglers) realised what an important species of fish this really is! Without the pike to stop the spread of disease, I fear there would probably eventually be no other fish! The presence of pike in our waters is not a bad sign, it is a very good sign and goes some way towards guaranteeing the health and survival of our fish stocks. The pike are not a threat to all other fish when the natural balance of nature is maintained. If they were then they would have wiped out all the other fish thousands of years ago. This however, is clearly not the case (nearly all species of fish are predators to some extent in the strictest sense of the word.) Predator and prey have lived in relative harmony since time began. Pike are not going to make all other species extinct any time soon!

Like I have previously stated: Pike keep their own numbers down. However, if pike continue to be culled, killed, taken or removed from our waters and eaten at the rate that they are being taken. Then the pike itself may become an endangered species. It is about time that these fish were treated with the respect that they deserve.

AN ABSOLUTE DISGRACE

Many years ago whilst visiting a local pond. I saw a large dead pike laying at the side of the bank. I asked one of the local fishermen about it. He told me that it had been caught and weighed at twenty five pounds, then tossed into the undergrowth and left to die a slow, agonising death on the bank, at the side of the pond, scorched to death in the mid-day summer sun, (and we say that pike are monsters!)

What's worse is that to many people, this wonderful, remarkable creature which was set at naught and so cruelly despised and discarded would have represented possibly the highlight of their fishing career. Their single best ever achievement, the capture of a lifetime - a specimen 'trophy' fish and quite possibly the culmination of a life times hard work and effort for someone more worthy of the title 'fisherman.'

As I have mentioned, carp eat fish too! Imagine the uproar if a pike fisherman treated a twenty five pound carp with such disdain! It would not be stood for and rightly so. A twenty five pound pike deserves MAXIMUM respect. They are there for a reason.

Another similiar story I heard about on the same water went thus. A car ended up in the pond. It was dragged out. Inside the car was found a pike of about twenty five pounds. Imagine how hard it is trying to catch a pike that has made a car its lair - snag city. Again, this wonderful specimen was needlessly slaughtered for no reason.

Need I remind these people that nearly ALL fish are predatory to a greater or lesser extent - pike, perch, carp, chub, trout, salmon, catfish, zander, they all eat fish! All of them! If we killed every fish that ate other fish then we would have no fish left to catch! What is the saying... "You can't teach stupid!"

BACKWARDS LOGIC!

Another time, I visited these two ponds that are back to back. "Which is the best pond to fish for pike?" I asked one of the local fishermen. He informed me that pond 1 is full of carp, Tench and coarse fish and that all the pike that are caught in pond 1 are taken out of pond 1 and put in pond 2. And to make sure that if I fished pond 1 for pike, and caught any, that I took them out, and put them in pond 2.

Pond 2 contains mainly pike taken from pond 1 and the odd perch! (Lucky perch!)

The next time I visited these two ponds I was told the following: If you catch any pike in pond 2 make sure that you put them back in pond 1. "Why is that?" I asked. "Because pond 1 is over run with stunted little fish and nobody can catch anything decent because we are terrorised and plagued by little fish nibbling at our bread and maggots." "Unbelievable!" I thought to myself, Isn't that what always happens when you mess with the balance of nature? Something goes wrong... What gives?

Another time I arrived at a lovely looking stretch of canal only to learn from one of the local bailiffs that they had already removed about TWO HUNDRED pike from the water that year and presumably moved them to who knows where...

Apparently, the environment agency 'advised' them to do it!

Brilliant!! What I would like to know is HOW they transported these TWO HUNDRED pike from the canal to the nearest water which is at least a quarter of a mile if not half a mile away on foot? I'll answer that for you shall I - they didn't! Given the complete disdain which they have for pike and their welfare and all the 'scrub' land in the area... My guess is that these pike's final resting place came to be at the bottom of the nearest thornbush! Was the - so called 'environment' agency there to witness this mickey mouse operation? I doubt it.

Sorry folks but when you hear about the environment agency guys clearing weed growth out of a local river or canal (supposedly to prevent flooding) and then see photos in your local paper of eels in the weed, left on the bank to die. it does not exactly inspire confidence does it? Oh, and I might add (just in case anybody didn't know) that eels are classed as an endangered species - an endangered species! What is the world coming to? If only somebody had told these incompetent bozos that! When you pay your licence fees I very much doubt that this money is being put to good use... I think it more likely that the millions of pounds that the sales of license fees generate each year is resting nicely in someones bank account. Environment agency - do your job.

TOUGH AS NAILS

The pike is a very hardy fish which possesses extremely efficient digestion and assimilation of food sources and the ability when nature requires to live a very spartan existence surviving on next to nothing for days or even weeks on end. As evidenced by the out of condition, practically starving pike that are caught 'long and lean' at certain times of the year such as autumn/winter. Or in particularly hard to live in waters where pike have practically nothing to live on besides each other, leeches (which also feed on the pike) and small insects, along with frogs in breeding season...

I know of a water like this: A small pond at the back of a golf course which contains a few small pike of one to four pounds in weight (possibly a few small fish) and practically no other food sources with the exception of leeches and microscopic water insects.

I also know of another water - a canal which is a nature reserve/wildlife sanctuary. This water is absolutely full and overrun with literally hundreds if not thousands of tiny pike which weigh on average less than a pound or just a few ounces in weight. There are a fair few pike of one to three pounds, a few weighing five pounds or more and a small handful or two of big pike of double figures or twenty pounds or so.

I have seen no other species of fish in this water except for pike. The only other creatures that live in this water in any numbers are frogs (in breeding season) and waterfowl. I can only deduce that the pike in this canal live an almost purely cannibalistic life style and eat an almost purely cannibalistic diet from a very young age.

I find it very hard to believe that any other small fish such as stickleback's, minnow's, roach or perch could survive in such a fierce and harsh environment. The life cycle of the pike in this scenario must then be as follows: The majority of the small pike that are born every year are eaten by the survivors of last years hatch and the year before that and so on...

In other words, the majority of the pike born every year in this particular water are literally fodder for last years few remaining survivors to feed upon. It is 'survival of the fittest' at it's most extreme. One dominant species of fish that survives by feeding on each other. The tiny newborn pike may find insects to feed upon before turning cannibal at a very young age as a necessity to ensure or 'maximise' their chances of survival. The slightly bigger pike of about a pound or so in weight may turn to eating frogs every year in breeding season to compliment their mainly cannibalistic diet. The bigger pike of about ten pounds or so may eat frogs, water voles/shrews or rats, ducklings, ducks, moorhens, coots, goslings or baby herons as well as any other birds or waterfowl that are readily available...

The pike is a universal hunter and opportunistic feeder with very catholic tastes. He will eat just about anything that looks like food. Hence why so many luminous, multicoloured, weird and wonderful lures get taken by pike every day even though they may resemble nothing that the pike has ever seen before, nothing that lives in his natural environment and indeed nothing in this world!

In my experience, having kept pike (and other native species of course fish) in tanks for many years, A newborn pike of less than one inch will reach roughly a pound in weight or a foot in length at the end of the first year. There is a lot of room for manoeuvre in this. If a pike has an 'abundance' of food readily available he may grow longer and heavier much faster. If there is literally nothing available to eat but bloodworms or other microscopic insects then the pike will stay alive/survive but in a permanently 'stunted' state, until more food becomes readily available and then they will begin to grow again. They could stay in a 'stunted' state measuring just a few centimetres for many weeks, months or possibly even years. This is true of all fish. They do not grow in proportion to their environment as some people naively believe but actually grow in direct proportion to readily available food sources.

In my opinion, this is the case with your pet goldfish... They are kept in an unnatural, artificially stunted state (goldfish bowl) fed goldfish flakes (mainly ash and next to nothing) and prevented from reaching their maximum size potential. Remember: Goldfish are members of the carp family and it is well known/documented that carp can live to about fifty odd years old and weigh over fifty pounds!

Curiously, just across the road from this canal is a river which contains lots of trout, grayling, chub, perch and barbel and just about every other species of course fish except the pike. It makes me wonder if all these pike were taken from the river which is a natural fishery and placed into the canal which is a man made feature. Hence why there are very few pike (practically none) in the river and literally thousands of pike (and no other species of fish) in the canal. This does seem an unnatural state of affairs but if this is the case (the pike were removed from the river so that the trout, grayling and other fish could thrive) then fine - at least they were given refuge/sanctuary in a nature reserve/ wildlife sanctuary and not just cruelly killed/discarded.

I know why this has most probably happened: Because they want the river to be for fly fishing for trout and grayling. This just doesn't make sense to me. Pike can be taken on the fly also...

I have caught trout and pike on the same day and I can tell you now that a take from a pike is much harder, more aggressive/exciting than a take from a trout of the same weight or similiar weight... The difference is incredible!

THE KING OF ALL FISH - A SPORT FISHERMAN'S DREAM COME TRUE

I only wish that everyone could and would recognize the pike for the amazing sport fish that he is, due to his ferocious, extremely aggressive nature and behaviour. I have seen pike jump clean out of the water in pursuit of surface poppers, topwater lures and artificial frogs. I have seen pike tail-walking and fight very athletically indeed - acrobatically even. I have seen pike jump out of the water in pursuit of other pike. I have seen pike move at speeds comparable to rockets going off on fireworks night. I have seen pike move at shocking speeds which could hardly be kept up with by the naked eye. I am not exaggerating. I speak the truth as a long time pike angler.

Anglers around the world are starting to recognise and realise what a select few have known all throughout history. It amazes me that people rate the trout as a better sport fish. I just don't see it. They are both aggressive and thus relatively easy to catch. They can both be caught by many methods including spinning and fly fishing.

There is however one main difference: The average pike is bigger than the average trout and also possesses a larger maximum size potential.
It is about time that the angling community woke up and opened their eyes to the great potential of pike fishing and took full advantage of the great opportunity to fish for this wonderful creature that lives on our doorstep and gets taken for granted and nowhere near enough respect. As for the true fishermen and pike lovers out there... As always, I salute you.

I think all of this originates from the attitude of the upper class in this country. They originally called coarse fishing 'coarse' fishing because the upper crust thought it was 'coarse.' Where as sport fishing for trout and salmon on the fly was seen as some how noble or honourable. I think all of this silly thinking is outdated and ignorant. In my humble opinion: The pike is the greatest 'sport' fish of all...

FLY FISHING FOR PIKE - THE PINNACLE OF OUR SPORT

In the future, I see the pike overtaking the trout in this country and others as the 'recognised' number one sport fish. I see fly fishing for pike taking over in popularity from fly fishing for trout. Mainly due to, as I said earlier the pike being a superior predator. Superior in speed, size, power, weight and aggression. As well as being readily available to fish for in waters all over the British Isles.

Indeed, I do not know why it was ever overlooked in the first place in favour of smaller fish. Fly fishing for pike is catching on all over the world and nobody can deny that pike flies are magnificent works of art and the tyers of pike flies are very talented and possess 'skilled' hands. I believe that catching pike on the fly represents the pinnacle of pike fishing and the future of our sport.

THE PIKE AND THE MATCH FISHERMAN

On the surface it would seem that pike and match fishermen are natural enemies. I know that some match fishermen regard pike as vermin and a nuisance. This is a very sad state of affairs in this day and age. It is my firm opinion that the match fishermen probably kill more fish (with their keep nets) than the pike do...

Seriously, it is completely unnatural (not to mention harmful and detrimental to the fishes health) to hoard tens if not hundreds of pounds of weight of shoal fish in a keep net for hours on end or all day long. Anyone who has ever kept fish in an aquarium knows that two of the biggest killers of fish are surprise surprise! OVERCROWDING and STRESS!

They might be alive (just) after you have finally weighed and released them but probably not for long. My guess is that at least half of them die in the wild after you have released them. In that case, the pike is not the match fishermen's enemy. The match fisherman is his own worst enemy! The match fisherman is the pikes best friend!

I have seen match fishermen release fish out of their keep nets at the end of a 'long' day... I watched as these fish lay bobbing upside down on the surface of the water (floating slowly downstream) just waiting to be eaten! A nice, easy meal for any passing predator! Now, there is some food for thought... I rest my case.

CHAPTER 9.
CATCHING PIKE
& PREDATORS
ON LURES

BE PREPARED...

The 'wise' fisherman does his preparation at the kitchen table, at home, in advance... The fool does his preparation last minute at the waters edge...

ALWAYS TRAVEL AS LIGHT AS POSSIBLE...

(When lure fishing) always try to travel as light as possible. Don't carry too much gear. I have been guilty of this one many times in the past...

I find that travelling "too heavy" is strength, and energy sapping and sucks the joy out of the whole fishing experience.

ONLY A FOOL CARRIES EVERYTHING BUT THE KITCHEN SINK...

I ought to know because for a long time I was that fool!

On some of my fishing expeditions I have taken everything but the kitchen sink. It gets exhausting! Sometimes by the time I have made it to my desired spot I am completely knackered, I cannot even be bothered to set up, and the last thing I want to do is fish!

On a hot summers day - you get exhausted and dehydrated very quickly. Carrying too much gear takes all the pleasure and enjoyment out of fishing. Travel light - you'll enjoy your fishing a lot more...

If you forgot to pack something essential then use your imagination and improvise like you did back in the day when you had a lot less kit and probably a lot more fun!

THE EXCEPTION TO THE RULE...

The one "ABSOLUTELY ESSENTIAL ITEM" and exception to this rule is your unhooking tool...

NEVER FORGET YOUR UNHOOKING TOOL!

UNHOOKING TOOLS

Keep a pair of pliers, forceps or a multi (unhooking) tool in a little pouch attached to your belt for ease of access when unhooking fish.

I like to carry an unhooking 'multi-tool' attached to my belt (sometimes two) for ease of access. I have dropped them in deep water on two separate occasions so I like to carry a spare. One on the left hand side and one on the right.

UNHOOKING PIKE (SAFELY.)

Use a leather, gardening or chainmail glove for unhooking pike to prevent cuts or abrasions.

"CHINNING" PIKE...

YOU HAVE GOT TO BE ABLE TO CHIN PIKE PROPERLY...

It is very important, so all pike angler's must learn how to do it correctly...

There are two ways to do it: One way is to slip two fingers (index and middle) inside just one gill...

The other way is to 'split' your index and middle finger and slip them both between two different gills (left and right.) Both ways are equally effective. I guess it just comes down to personal preference.

The trick is not to accidently slip your fingers between the gill rakers (the rough, sharp, red bits hidden inside the gills) as these will cut your hands/fingers. The gill rakers are designed that way, so that prey fish cannot escape or swim out of the gills when a pike strikes or 'takes' a prey fish head first.

If you can chin pike (it gets very easy with practise and experience) then you can unhook them with the greatest of ease and convenience. The more pike you catch - the more practise you will get.

Initially, I would ask an experienced pike angler to show you how to do it...

If you don't know anybody then watch a tutorial on the internet (on youtube.) Like everything else: It is easy when you know how.

At the end of the day: If you cannot unhook pike properly then you have no business fishing for them!

UNHOOKING 'DEEP HOOKED' PERCH

If a perch ever gets deep hooked due to 'inhaling' a spinner which does happen very occasionally. It has happened to me once or twice... I would simply unclip the wire trace and unhook by feeding the spinner (and trace) out through one of the gills (the nearest one.) I have done this before and it was simple and straightforward (the fish were fine) and there were no issues/ problems unhooking in this way.

NEVER FORGET YOUR WIRE TRACES!

WIRE TRACES

Hang a few wire traces, clipped around your waist on the little bits of fabric that hold your belt in place. For quick, easy and convenient access. Just loop them around in circles and clip them each to themselves.

Also, the long, clear plastic tubes you get for your kids (for blowing bubble mixture) are ideal storing tubes for storing longer wire traces in.

Also, don't forget fluids to keep you hydrated and sugary snacks to keep your blood sugar and energy levels up.

One time me and my fishing buddy went dead baiting and when we got to our desired location we realised that we had no treble hooks and no floats! I know, I know, but it was a last minute thing and I had left my dead baiting kit in my other bag! I solved the riddle by improvising some treble hooks by attaching three large, single coarse fishing hooks together into makeshift treble hooks and improvised a pike float out of a plastic bottle, and yes, miraculously, we did catch a pike on this hodgepodge of a rig!

Always carry a waterproof bag (in case it rains heavily or the bag falls in the water) and use waterproof boxes and compartments for storing lures. Tins can be very useful for storing tackle and lures but are inferior as they can go rusty if allowed to get wet. I like to clip/attach my bag to saplings and bushes to stop my bag from rolling down steep banks into the water.

Polarised glasses can be very useful for seeing through surface glare on the water when lure fishing and stalking big fish - especially on rivers and canals.

FULL CAMO

Wear army camouflage gear as it is much harder to be seen/ noticed by fish and has lots of big, handy pockets for storing lures, plugs, spinners, spoons and useful bits and bobs.

FISHING RODS FOR LURE FISHING

ROD LENGTH

For casting lures, I recommend a stiff, strong, powerful rod of at least 6ft up to a maximum of 9ft. The longer the better for casting long distances with relatively light lures such as spinners or shallow diving minnow type lures. However, I personally never go above 9 feet in length as I find 9 feet to be the ideal length for me (I am 5ft 7 inches tall.) Someone who is taller may prefer a longer rod of 10 ft plus and somebody shorter may prefer a shorter rod of 6 - 8 ft in length. The choice is yours... For casting heavy dead baits a solid twelve foot rod ensures maximum casting distance.

ROD STRENGTH

Ultra light, flimsy, bendy, overflexible rods are not very good for casting long distances due to the flexibility of the rod acting like a shock absorber and thus greatly reducing casting distance. I like to use a two and a half to three pound test curve rod for my pike fishing. I would not recommend anything below a two pound test curve or above a three pound test curve for the majority of pike fishing. A flimsy rod whilst giving great pleasure and maximum sport whilst playing modest fish could snap in half if you hook a twenty or thirty pound pike or big catfish unexpectedly. Also, a flimsy rod is not suitable (or practical) for repeatedly casting heavy lures or deadbaits long distances. I have used short (6 - 7ft) sea fishing/boatfishing type rods for lure fishing/pike fishing in the past. They tend to be very strong, durable and reliable. Ideal for repetitive casting of lures/deadbaits and playing heavy fish. If you are considering buying or using a seafishing/boatfishing rod for your lure fishing/pike fishing just bear in mind that some of them although very tough and practically indestructable, can be heavy and hard work to carry and repeatedly cast out lures all day long with.

My advice: Lighter is always better and I don't mean test curve. I mean the actual physical weight of the rod. buying a rod is a personal thing. Buy the rod that you fall in love with, a rod that will be a pleasure to fish with. Buy the best that you can afford and always use the right tool for the job. Have you ever heard the saying: Buy cheap - buy twice!

THE FIRST CAST...

The first cast you make in any peg, spot, stretch of river, or canal is always the most important. Always remember that, because you do not always get a second chance at a big fish. The first cast is your best chance of catching any fish in your peg or swim. The first cast of a lure or bait is so effective because more often than not the fish have not cottoned onto the fact that you are there and thus are in their element. Behaving in exactly the way that they would in their natural environment (as if you were not there at all.) You must take advantage of this and capitalise on your golden opportunity...

CASTING LURES

Learn to use, rely on and perfect THE SIDE CAST - for greater casting accuracy when repetitively casting lures. The overhead cast is second class when it comes to lure fishing. You want to be a first class (lure) fisherman, not a second class one. Using the 'side cast' allows you much greater casting accuracy when putting your lures in particularly hard to reach spots and makes you more of a 'hot shot' (like me.)

SETTING YOUR DRAG CORRECTLY

Always set the drag on your reel correctly so as to set the hook properly and be able to give line simultaneously. Set it too loosely and it will give line when you strike, thus losing you fish. Set it too tightly and you risk being snapped off in the heat of the moment when playing your dream fish.

RECOVERING LURES...

<u>DEALING WITH TREE/BRANCH SNAGS...</u>

Timing/looping a snagged lure over a tree branch (exactly the same way that it went over the branch) but backwards or in reverse... (Think of the 'visual' when pressing rewind on a video recorder.)

If you cast your lure over a tree branch and you are quick enough you can pull it back the opposite way in exactly the same motion that it went over the branch using an almost 'pendulum' swing like motion. I have done this many times and now have it down to an almost art form.

Once mastered, it is a very useful and reliable way to recover your lures from tree branches. Use a quick 'twitch' of your rod tip to free lures as soon as they go over a tree branch... Precise timing is necessary/ideal to use the momentum of the lure swing to pull it back over the branch before it comes to a complete stop. Also, don't use too much force or pull too hard. Just enough is all you need...

<u>DEALING WITH RIVER/CANAL BED SNAGS...</u>

when your lure is snagged on the bottom of a river/canal... Walking up or down river/canal (a dozen feet or more) past the snagged lure and pulling your lure in the opposite direction can often free up your lure in an otherwise hopeless situation.

Always remember to re-set reel clutch drag after tightening up on super tough snags...

<u>OPTIMALLY FILLING YOUR REEL SPOOL</u>

Fill your spool with line correctly to maximise casting distance on big waters. However, do not overfill your spool as this will cause bird's nests (tangles.) Fill it to within one or two mm of being flush with the rim of the spool. If you are experiencing bird's nests then you have either overfilled your spool or are using cheap, poor quality line. In which case replace it asap. I prefer to use 'deep' reel spools which hold more line, and which contribute to greater casting distance and more lure 'exposure' in the strike zone...

STRIKING...

STRIKING EFFECTIVELY

When lure fishing for pike, zander, trout or salmon striking is very important. As any experienced pike fisherman will tell you a pike's mouth is "all teeth and bone" thus a pike - large or small can be very difficult to hook without sharp, high quality hooks and a fast, accurate, hard strike. Some pike fishermen always strike twice to be doubly sure of hooking the fish. Some fishermen strike upwards, some to the side, some diagonally (upwards and to the side.) I tend to strike to the side and wind the reel handle quickly (2 or 3 times simultaneously.) Striking to the side isn't the hardest type of strike but I value my eyesight and don't particularly like dodging flying 'head hunting' lures and trebles! The only exception to this is when I am live or deadbaiting in this case I will strike upwards 'HARD' and really bend into the fish to maximise hook penetration, it sounds cruel but when fishing for these 'prehistoric monsters' you really need to maximise the chances of a good hook hold...

PLAYING BIG FISH...

SIDE STRAIN

When playing big fish. Pulling upwards and applying to much pressure too soon to a fresh, strong, hard-fighting fish may result in the hooks being pulled clean out of the fish's mouth and flying directly back at you! It is usually much safer to apply sidestrain to the fish (pull from the side to the left or right with rod tip held low preferably as low as possible and pointing at the surface of the water.) This means that there is less chance of you pulling the hooks out of the fish's mouth and less chance of you having to duck and dodge flying lures and/or trebles.

LINE TENSION

I will let you in on a little secret... When you have struck on and made first contact with a big fish, you do not have to be retrieving line or physically reeling in the fish to be making progress, playing or tiring a big fish. No, in fact sometimes, attempting to heave in or bully in a big, strong, fresh and vigorous fish can be the biggest mistake you could ever make. This is how line breakages and fish jumping clear out of the water and throwing the hooks occur. Sometimes the best thing to do is to bend your rod into the fish to maintain tension on the line (keeping the hooks set) and attempt to tire or play the fish without using the reel or with minimal or slow reel wind. It is better to play a big fish out in the open water than to feel his power and realise your mistake when it is too late at the side of the bank when you try to net a fish that is full of beans and ultra lively. The fish will see you and the net and panic and start taking off on runs...

ALWAYS EXPECT AT LEAST 3 OR 4 GOOD RUNS...

Always expect a pike of ten pounds or double figures to be capable of at least three or four runs before tiring out and slipping into the net. A really big pike may make five or six runs...

YOU HAVE TO TIRE EM OUT...

Don't try to land the fish before you have played him (or her) properly and tired them out... If the pike goes in the net without giving a good account of itself and taking off on at least three good runs then - oh well, at least you were prepared. The day WILL COME when you hook a pike that is well capable of going on at least 3 or 4 if not 5 or 6 spectacular, gill flaring, head thrashing, tail walking runs...

Then it is important that you...

NEVER LOSE YOUR COOL IN THE HEAT OF THE MOMENT AND TRY TO BULLY IN A BIG FISH...

RELAX, BE COOL, STAY CALM, TAKE YOUR TIME...

BETTER TO LAND IT EVENTUALLY - EVEN IF IT TAKES YOU HALF AN HOUR (VERY UNLIKELY) THAN NEVER TO LAND IT AT ALL

You would be surprised how often this happens. An experienced fisherman hooks the fish of a lifetime (a personal best) and then in the heat of the moment forgets everything he ever knew about fishing and completely blows it...

The result can be very disappointing...

I once caught a five foot long, forty pound plus catfish on (sylcast) nine pound breaking strain line! If I had tried to bully in that fish I would have lost it (guaranteed.)

When a big fish comes up to the top or surface of the water, stops 'fighting hard' and trying to run and lays on its side. That usually indicates that it is ripe for netting!

FRONT AND REAR DRAG

Make sure your drag is set correctly and your reel does what it is supposed to when it's supposed to. If a big fish does take off on a run and your drag does kick in and the fish is stripping line off the reel - don't worry or panic . As long as you have plenty of line on your spool and you maintain contact with the fish, ultimately he is still hooked and he is still on so just stay calm, relax, take your time and let your rod and reel do their job, just maintain line tension all of the time by bending into the fish and recover line gradually little by little, bit by bit, over the course of the battle...

BACK TO LURE FISHING...

Wear a wide brimmed hat or peaked cap to help keep the sun out of your eyes while surveying the water...

The Golden Rule:

ALWAYS WATCH YOUR LURE WHILST RETRIEVING IT IN THE WATER...

NEVER TAKE YOUR EYES OFF YOUR LURE!

HEADS UP - A BIG PIKE TAKES A POP AT MY SHOE HORN SPINNER

One day, I came up with the ingenious idea of turning a silvery, chrome coloured, (old man's) shoe horn into an 'oversized' pike spinner. I taped holographic silver tape to the big 'blade' of the spinner on both sides. The result was a lure so big, loud, bright and obvious that it could be seen spinning from the moon or outer space! Just as I intended. I took it down to a likely spot of the Trent canal where there were a few pike lurking about. The water on this particular stretch of canal is so deep and dark as to be almost black. I cast out a few times and made the classic mistake of not paying enough attention to my lure. Unbeknownst to me, something else was paying attention... At the last possible second, as I was pulling my shoehorn spinner out of the water to re-cast it into my swim a large pike's head came up and out of the water after my lure, like a miniature recreation of a scene for the shark movie jaws! The pike missed my lure by less than a second! I cast out my lure again, many more times but never saw that big pike again. If I had been paying more attention, and slowed down the retrieve of my lure (just a fraction) towards the end of my go, right before I intended to cast out again I might - might just have caught that pike! The moral of the story: STAY 'SWITCHED ON' AND...

ALWAYS PAY ATTENTION TO YOUR LURES!!!

pike takes are F-A-S-T!
If you become distracted and take your eye of the ball even for a second you may miss the fish of a lifetime! Don't believe me? A pike has the ability to take and REJECT a lure (or pike fly) in the time it takes you to blink! A curious but wary pike may follow, then take, then reject a hard, wood, plastic or metal lure in the time it takes you to sneeze! He could follow, then take and reject your lure (or fly) all in a split second and you might be none the wiser! pike are the fastest swimming freshwater fish on earth - reaching speeds of up to 40km!

A pike is by nature a very curious fish. He may take a lure or fly just to see what it is or to see if it's edible. A pike does not have hands to feel things with. All his investigating is done with his mouth! A soft jelly lure or shad may feel like food to a hungry pike but a hard lure certainly does not! Thus it will be rejected instantly, if it does not feel quite right.

If you cannot see your lure in the water then watch the exact point where your line enters the water or watch your rod tip... I like to hold my rod tip (low down) just above the surface of the water or even point the rod tip straight at the lure (if you tend to strike upwards.) If I am trying to make my lure swim high up on the top/surface of the water then I will hold the rod tip high up or even hold the rod vertically pointing straight up in the air (to guide the lure up to the surface of the water and take advantage of the pike's binocular vision.)

<u>USING THE FIGURE OF EIGHT OR LURE 'CIRCLING'</u>

This piece of advice can be useful for fishing from the bank or from a boat out on the water...

Sometimes when you are lure fishing you get a follow from a

very interested, 'keen' pike that follows your lure all the way to the bank and you almost run out of line... Don't reel in until you completely run out of line! Keep at least five or six feet or a full 'rod's length' of line between the tip of the rod and your lure... Then 'circle' the lure around and around in front of you or move your lure in a figure of eight 'pattern' until either you get a take or the fish loses interest (hopefully you get a take.)

I once caught a nice pike that was 'hanging around' in my swim directly below and in front of me simply by 'circling' or rotating my lure around, and around in circles (different directions) until I got a nice (fully committed) take... Believe it or not (when the pike is hungry, has 'tunnel vision' and is fully 'fixated' on your lure... This method can be very successful! (When done right.) Once again, experience counts... practise makes perfect, and success begets assurance. Just because a pike has seen you doesn't mean he wont commit. Sometimes, they do! Their instinct or 'prey drive' is so strong it can override everything else! Luckily for us!

<u>LURES</u>

Have faith in your lures - no matter how cheap, simple, primitive or basic and even if you have never caught on that particular type, colour, make or model of lure before. There's a first time for everything and most lures will catch fish at one time or another. So have faith in your lures and yourself. If you don't believe in them, then they won't work. It's only a piece of wood, metal or plastic after all and it's up to your skill and imagination to bring your lures to life. If you can believe in yourself and them, then maybe the fish can too but if even you don't believe in them, then how's the fish gonna believe in them. I first caught a pike on a homemade spinner twenty six years ago (when I was eighteen years old.) I was catching pike twenty years ago on home made surface plugs (no dive) made from nothing more than three or four inches of broomstick handle, pvcu tape, curtain eyes and drawing pins for fish eyes (from wilkos.) If you can believe then you can achieve. What one man can do - another can do. I have caught a pike using only an ordinary wine bottle cork as a lure. I did this to show my friends that it could be done and it didn't take long either and I have even fooled a wild, fifteen pound mirror carp into taking a modified plug that I had altered and tampered about with and this was over twenty years ago. I know A LOT more now than I did back then.

MAKE YOUR OWN SURFACE POPPERS

From three - four inches of broom stick handle, some green, yellow, red, white or black pvcu tape, or bright shiny holographic sticky back paper, model eyes or drawing pins for eyes and curtain eyes to attach your hooks and wire trace. Keep it simple and use your imagination... Some good patterns are dark geen and black stripes. Yellow and black stripes. Red head (one third) and white body (two thirds). Red head and yellow body (same as above). Black head, white body. Plain black or plain white. With red, yellow or green drawing pins for eyes. Trust me - these work! I have caught plenty of pike on these simple plugs and you can make them in minutes...

Don't make the classic mistake of buying hundreds of lures. Buy the best designed and best quality lures that you can afford. Don't get me wrong - there is nothing wrong with cheap, good quality, reliable, value for money lures, nothing at all. It's just that eventually you will end up with lots and lots of different lures that take up lots of space and require a lot of organising. Take it from me - I know! It gets even worse once you start making your own spinners, spoons and plugs!

Lures generally fall into four categories...

1.Great lures - The best of the best "old faithfuls." 1st choice, Top quality, tried and tested, fish takers and catchers that you can place 100% faith in on almost any water. (These tend to be the tatty old plugs or spoons that are covered in teeth marks.) The type of lure that you wish you had bought half a dozen of instead of just the one! And, if you lose them, then you are left scouring the earth to try and replace them

2. Good lures - need I say more?

3. Okay lures or so/so lures - Acceptable lures that can catch fish in skillful hands in the right conditions on the right day.

4. crap lures. Ones that looked good in the shop window or the catalogue or when you were shopping online. But never measured up when put to the test. Lures that were badly designed, mass produced and cheaply made. The lures that you never seem to catch on no matter how hard you try! The ones you wish you hadn't bought! The ones you wish that you had left in the shop window... Basically - the ones that you always leave at home when you go fishing!

E.G. spinners that don't spin! Or only spin in a fast current or when reeled against the current but don't spin when reeled in with the current or in still water. Or spinners that aren't 100% reliable. Or spinners that only spin on 8 out of 10 casts because the spinner blade keeps wrapping around the wire shank of the spinner! You know the ones I'm talking about! I don't care how long they've been around! That's the amazing thing! They have been around for all these years and they still haven't been fixed! Do these people even fish? Or actually test their products? My advice: If your spinners don't spin, break them down and rebuild them yourself.

It is better to own a dozen old faithfuls (great lures) than a hundred unknown quantities (crap lures.) It's like friends - better one true friend than a thousand false ones. And for the same reason: THEY WILL LET YOU DOWN WHEN YOU NEED

THEM MOST! I.E on the riverbank.

LURE COLOURS

Seeing red! Pike and perch are suckers for the colour red. ..
Red spinners, spoons, diving plugs and surface lures are all great fish catchers.

Gold, silver, green, yellow, red, white, blue and black are good colours for plugs.

Gold, silver, copper, red and green are all good colours for spinners.

Gold, silver, copper and blue are all good colours for spoons.

Never be afraid to experiment with lures and always trust your gut instincts.

USING SPINNERS

Somebody once said about Rocky Marciano the undefeated, heavyweight boxing champion of the world "He ain't pretty - he's just devastating!" Well spinners are pretty and equally devastating! Just try one!

The humble spinner is an often overlooked but very effective, versatile and reliable lure. A consistent catcher in all types of waters, in any weather conditions from clear to flood water conditions and for many species of predatory fish including but not limited to pike, perch, trout, salmon, chub and zander. A lure which is literally 'deadly' in silver, gold and copper for pike, perch and trout. The Humble Spinner has been around for decades if not centuries and it is probably due to this fact that it has been so taken for granted and overlooked in modern lure fishing. Indeed with it's combination of brightness, colour, sound and vibration plus its ability to imitate both distressed, fleeing prey fish and fly it is hard to improve upon and hard to beat!

Another advantage of fishing with a spinner, is that they are compact and aerodynamic, making them easy to cast long distances. Yet another great thing about spinners is that although they are a small lure, they create a big disturbance underwater, thus making them seem like a bigger meal than they really are.

If you said to me (a very experienced lure fisherman and predator specialist who has been fishing for over thirty years with hundreds, maybe thousands of captures under his belt.) "You can go fishing today but only take one box of lures." I'd take a small box of spinners from 10 to 15 grams each in weight...

If you said "pick 2 spinners." I'd take a 10 gram silver and a 10 gram golden spinner out with me. If you said "pick one spinner." It would be a tough decision as they are both very effective spinners on their day but I would have to favour a 10 gram golden spinner. 15 grams is at the maximum (heavy) end for a pike spinner. 12 grams may be more optimum. If I was fishing for perch, chub, trout or zander then 10 or 12 grams would be sufficient. If casting distance wasn't important then 10 grams would be optimum. If you need to cast further out then 12 grams is useful for that.

I have fished big lakes where pike won't take a plug with any consistency. Where big pike ignore or refuse to hit ANY type of plug. They follow them and eye them up suspiciously! They hit the spinners though, you simply can't catch on any other lure than a spinner on waters like that. I've fished canals where spinners have out-fished plugs for pike and perch. I've used nothing but spinners all day on a river/chalkstream for trout and had literally hundreds of hits, knocks and takes. If you are new to lure fishing for predators, trust me, spinners do the business... they are reliable and consistent fish catchers... Especially gold, silver and copper.

Another good thing about using spinners when fishing for soft mouthed species such as perch or chub is that you don't really have to strike very hard - the fish pretty much hooks itself on the take! Especially perch - perch inhale the spinner!

FAVOURITE COLOURS

Silver - Nothing beats a small (10 grams) silver spinner! It is often my 1st choice as it imitates such a wide variety of species of fish such as roach, rudd, dace, chub, barbel, gudgeon, common and rainbow trout, grayling, loach and other 'silvery' coloured fish species.

A silver spinner is always a good choice in any water conditions from crystal clear to murky water but especially effective (due to high visibility) in wet, rainy, murky water conditions and especially for catching big and highly predatory chub (in the three - five pound plus region) and perch (in the two - three pound plus region.)

Both species love to predate on the young fry and offspring of fish which tend to be predominantly silver in colour and both fish hunt confidently in rainy, murky water conditions. Chub love to hunt in dark, cloudy, murky water due to their (relatively) 'shy' nature. Believe it or not, I have caught several large, lake chub (4 or 5 pounds plus) on home-made spinners made out of table spoons!

Copper or brass coloured - again highly recommended! An absolute winner... Big pike and big perch love copper coloured spinners.

Red - Imitating young perch and juvenile pike (perch and pike have bright red fins and tails) blood or a wounded, injured or dying fish. Red is a particularly good colour for catching perch (which love to feed on perch) and of course pike (which love to feed on pike and perch too.)

Gold - Again lots of fish 'hybrids' are a goldy colour - roach, rudd, bream...

Gold spinners are second to none and show up very well in discoloured or brown 'muddy' water.

Luminous - **yellow**, **green**, **orange** and **pink** which imitates nothing in this world except perhaps a goldfish or a golden orfe, fly or dragonfly. Again, highly recommended and have accounted for captures of many pike, perch and trout. Perch and trout especially seem to go for bright, luminous and unnaturally bright colours.

The silver, lightweight mackerel spinner is a dynamite lure! it is absolutely deadly for trout. I have caught trout all day long on just that one lure with no need to change lures - it is very efficient. The only problem is that they are a bit 'light weight' probably weighing only 6 - 8 grams. Thus limiting casting distance considerably.

FOUR METHODS OF USING SPINNERS

1. Slow, steady and 'constant' retrieve spinning to incite a follow and take or a 'swirl' (one hundred and eighty degrees take.)

2. Deep spinning or slow retrieve spinning - skimming the bottom of the river bed or lake bottom for big pike, perch or trout laying on the bottom. You have to beware of snags using this method.

3. Pointing your rod up in the air or holding your rod higher up and retrieving your spinner across the surface of the water to create a big, dramatic bow - wave, (thus representing a bigger bait.)

4. Stop/start spinning - creating a big disturbance underwater.

THE BIG SPLASH - SURFACE POPPERS - HOW IT ALL BEGAN...

About twenty years ago, I was pike fishing on a big lake (as usual.) I got snapped off on a snag and lost my diving lure so I started rooting about in my tackle box for another lure. I didn't have many lures on me that day (which is very unusual for me) and it was slim pickings. Due to me not having any of my old faithfuls on me, I decided to try a top water lure or 'surface' popper (a flat faced lure with no dive at the front.) Even though I owned some of them, I had kind of forgotten about them and had not used them for about four years! I put one on and cast out to my left, underneath a big tree. I got a take - 1st cast! I reeled in a pike of about 5lbs. After that, I caught three more pike in quick succession on my surface popper that night. There's something in this, I thought to myself. Me and my brother came back and fished the same lake. Yet again, on surface poppers. It was 8.30pm at night when we started fishing and we got ten takes in an hour and a half! All from pike, except one huge, specimen perch. A perch that came all the way up from the bottom on a deep lake and took a four inch home made surface popper! This has happened to me again on a super deep lake. It made a believer out of me! As I was to learn, this was just a run of the mill day when fishing using surface poppers.

Surface poppers are one of the most versatile and effective lures on the market. They are brilliant in shallow rivers, ponds and lakes. Great for using on weedy rivers and ponds when you cannot even run a spinner, spoon or diving, sub-surface lure through the water on account of the weed. They just slide, smoothly over the top and bring the pike and perch out of their holes. Me and my buddies have caught so many pike on surface poppers that I have lost count! Fishing deep water or shallow water they take them just the same. To be honest with you, this is probably some of the most exciting fishing known to man. You get huge bow - waves following your popper, pike leaping out of the water like salmon, pike jumping out of the water like great whites or killer whales taking seals. If you have never tried them before then you are in for a big treat! Just trust me, oh boy, do they work! It's the pike's binocular vision you see, eyes at the top and front of his head... He's made to hunt and catch prey on the surface of the water as well as under the water. Frogs, toads, newts, river rats, water voles, small birds and mammals, whatever... He's not fussy. Anything for a bit of sport and an easy meal. What really gets the pike's juices flowing is the splashing, the disturbance, the commotion, the more fuss and noise the better! You see, to a hungry pike splashing represents struggling - something that is not meant to be in the water, that has fallen into the water and is struggling to swim and to stay afloat and not drown. This represents the easiest of easy meals. To a hungry pike - splashing means movement and movement means life and life means food. To a hungry pike splashing means vulnerability - that his prey is a lot slower and less mobile than he is and thus an easy target, a guaranteed meal - maximum reward for minimum effort.

Chub love surface poppers too... Especially river chub. Perch and trout take them too but it is better to use smaller ones for trout on account of their smaller mouths. It doesn't matter so much for chub and perch - they have got mouth's like buckets anyway.

I once caught a pike using nothing other than a wine bottle cork for a surface lure - for a bet and just to prove to myself that I could. My theory was proved correct... The movement of the lure is just as important as the appearance...

One of the best types of surface poppers are the ones with the transparant plastic propeller or 'blade' on the back... I used to own a luminous green rapala one, It was a reliable, fish taking lure before I retired it in a tree! You don't have to buy expensive lures, you can buy the cheap packs of three from aldi or lidl or better still just make some yourself like I do!

<u>FIVE METHODS OF TOPWATER LURE 'SURFACE' POPPING</u>

1. The rolling side to side retrieve...

This is probably the simplest and most effective method of

surface popping. All you do is cast out as far as you can, and then reel in a straight line, with a slow, steady retrieve. The idea is to give you're popper a lovely side to side roll or wobble on the surface of the water, which is irresistable to pike and predators. Just reel it in slow and steady and think "nice, easy, target." Simple! You can't go wrong.

2. The stop/start retrieve - fly fishing style... Again, this is an equally effective technique and just as easy. Just cast out as far as you can, then wait a few seconds for the ripples to spread out, then twitch your rod tip, then reel in the slack, twitch and reel, twitch and reel. Wanna mix it up a bit? twitch, and reel once, twitch and reel twice, twitch and reel three times, twitch and reel twice, twitch and reel once, pause, twitch and reel four times... oh, oh you better strike! Somethings just took your plug!!

Alternatively. Don't twitch you're rod tip at all, just reel in your line, at three alternate speeds - fast -slow - medium - stop - slow - medium - fast - stop - medium - fast - slow - stop - medium - slow - fast stop etc etc. There really are no hard and fast rules, Just use your imagination and have fun!

Or Just reel in with no rod tip twitch at all...

Reel once slow, reel twice fast, reel three times medium, stop. Reel four times slow, reel five times as fast as you can... Just mix it up and have fun - make it unpredictable.

3. Splashing - creating maximum noise, commotion and disturbance on the surface of the water...

Again, just cast out as far as you can, give it a few seconds for the ripples to spread out on the surface of the water and then start to retrieve. Give the rod tip a good, hard yank - like a mini strike - create a big splash, reel in five times rapidly, give your rod a good, hard yank, reel in again. Once again, there are no rules and there are no experts. The name of the game is noise and commotion, **you are simply trying to lure a big predator out of the shadows**

with the promise of an easy meal. Try to make as much of a fuss as you can on the surface of the water - make your lure stand out a mile off and make it o-b-v-i-o-u-s!!!!!

4. The s-l-o-w retrieve... I use this one for night time fishing, at dusk and in low light conditions. Cast out as far as you can, leave the lure resting on the surface of the water for ten seconds (or more) while the ripples spread out, and then begin your rolling side to side retrieve as s-l-o-w-l-y as possible - simple. The idea is to give the pike or predator the maximum amount of time to home in on and take your lure.

5. The fast retrieve... Again, cast out as far as you can, let the dust settle and then reel your popper in quickly or as fast as you can! This is a good method for fishing crystal clear water on a sunny, summers day... Or where the fish are particularly wise or cautious. The idea is not to let the pike get a chance to see what he is taking! If the lure is moving quickly it appears to be prey trying to flee and escape from danger. The pike or predator does not have time to make an informed decision. You are forcing his hand, he has to react quickly, it's now or never, he must take it or leave it. Last chance, make your move. He may snatch it instinctively before it gets away. The other thing that this method is good for is getting pike, chub or trout to give their positions away by chasing (tell tale bow wave or swirl) or striking at and missing your lure thus giving you the vital information you need about their whereabouts. Half the battle is finding the fishes whereabouts - location, location, location... Simply cast out again (it doesn't have to be the same lure, it could be a more realistic lure such as a Replica or any lure) into the same position and reel a little slower. Bang! you're in business this time!!

THE BEST TIME OF YEAR FOR USING SURFACE POPPERS

The best time of year to fish with surface poppers is from the beginning of May until the end of September. Basically the summer months - the hottest months of the year, when the sun is out, the weather is fine and the temperature is warm.

THE BEST TIMES OF DAY TO FISH WITH SURFACE POPPERS

The best time of day to fish with surface poppers is without a doubt in the evening. In the late evening just before sunset is the best time of day. After five pm is okay. After six is better. After seven, eight or nine is about prime time. Depending on the time of year and the length of day. Basically, during the last two or three hours of sunlight is the best time to use surface poppers. The other 'alternative' best time to use surface poppers is either at first light or in the morning. After 12pm it's time to switch to something else. I don't know why that is - it's just the way it is.

The only exceptions to these rules are when you are fishing water that is either 1. Too shallow or snaggy to use anything else such as shallow sections of rivers, ponds or lakes.

2. Too weedy to use anything else such as overgrown, weedy rivers, ponds or lakes. In these cases surface poppers may be the only 'safe' option.

ERRATIC STYLE LURE FISHING

Another time, me and another lad were fishing the same pond using small, bright, luminous green and orange, minnow type, diving plugs. My friend was catching more perch than me. "What are you doing that I'm not?" I asked. "Watch this" he said. It was then that I noticed the unusual style that he was fishing his lures. I had been casting them out and reeling them in steadily in a straight line - which caught me the odd perch. My friend was casting them out and reeling them in more quickly whilst simultaneously twitching his rod tip in between turns of the reel handle. The style of retrieving his lures that he was using is what I could only describe as frenzied and erratic. It was as if he was careless and not even trying to reel the lure in - in a lifelike and realistic manner. The movements of his lures were completely un-natural, and unpredictable as well as fast - I was surprised that the perch could catch them - but they were, and what's more this style of retrieve seemed to work better than what I was doing and was provoking some ferocious takes. Since then I have experimented with this 'erratic' style of lure fishing and found that it will induce takes especially from perch and trout when other styles of retrieve simply will not. It seems to irritate them. Put simply it PROVOKES the fish into attacking the lure! The more erratic, frenzied, and unpredictable the better.

With hindsight, I do think that this style of retrieve does imitate something... It imitates a distressed, panic stricken, prey fish that is frightened out of its wits, desperately fleeing, swimming for its life - trying to escape a big predator! Don't be afraid to work the lure up and down in different levels of water within one and the same cast. Try it - it works! Perch and trout are absolute suckers for bright, unnatural looking, luminous yellow, green, orange, red and pink spinners and plugs - the brighter, the better.

MINIATURE REPLICAS

Pike, perch, trout and chub also like ultra realistic, miniature replicas of other fish such as minnows, bullheads, baby trout, small perch and jack pike. I prefer the plastic ones to the rubber ones... You can fish with great confidence using these specimen taking high quality lures.

I have a rule I use in my lure fishing... If the water is crystal clear then I favour ultra realistic imitation lures such as the ones Salmo make... Imitations of native species of coarse fish such as carp, pike, perch, trout, bullhead, minnow, stickleback etc.

I am not affiliated with any lure company. I have no sponsors. After all these years fishing, I take pride in making my own fishing lures (I have done for 20 years!) and to be honest some of them are dynamite and cannot be outfished. I have made my own spinners, spoons, plugs, 'surface poppers' or top-water lures, duck lures, rat lures, frog/toad lures, hybrid lures, fly's (you name it - I've tried it!.)

Rapala have been around a long time and make some good lures that specialise in or emphasise realistic fish 'movement' which is very important. They make good elongated 'minnow' shape/type lures as well as others. It can get very expensive if you lose one in a tree or on a snag but they are top quality, reliable lures.

'propellor' (surface) lures... I am talking about those surface lures with a built in clear plastic 'blade' or propellor that spins around noisily at the back. Creating a popping or 'chugging' noise as you reel them in... Again, they are very good but rather expensive!

Abu Garcia also make some good lures (the tormentor) is one of them. The large ondex (silver and gold) spinners are especially good lures for big chub...

Mepps spinners are an old 'classic.' They have been around a long time and are nice, weighty (for casting) reliable fish takers...

Nowadays, with the arrival of the internet and online shopping - there are far too many good lure makers for me to remember or specifically mention. These are just a few.

Moving away from specific names or makes of lures. If the water conditions are not so favourable then I move over to the opposite end of the lure spectrum... Favouring the out of this world, wild and wacky, weird and wonderful, big, bright (can be seen from outer space) type of lures. Of the bright orange (goldfish colour) luminous yellow, luminous green, orange, red or pink variety.

BIG 'GAME' LURES

Usually, I like to tempt predators on small lures such as the above aforementioned, 10 gram gold and silver spinners or one of my homemade creations...

One time, I was fishing an unfamiliar river, downstream of a big waterfall/weirpool on lures and the water was deep and a bit discoloured (slightly less than optimum conditions for visibility) My 'old faithfuls' (trusty spinners) were not working! I mean zero takes - nothing. So, out of sheer frustration and desperation, I went to the opposite extreme and tried a bright, luminous orange and yellow 'bulldawg' of the rather large variety. Including the long, wriggly, rubber tail bit at the end, it was about a foot long! After only a few casts my lure was dramatically engulfed (out of the blue) right in front of me by a huge pike. This pike had a large head and a huge mouth and was probably the largest pike that I have ever seen attack/take a lure in real life at close range! It was about three feet long and 20 pounds in weight. That pike gave me an absolute battle and taught me a very important lesson that day...

I learned that...

BIGGER LURES ATTRACT BIGGER FISH...

One of the biggest mistakes I made for a long time was being reluctant to use big/bigger or really 'big' lures... I preferred the shallow diving, minnow shape, lures of about 4 inches in length. I had a lot of success on these but mainly from jack pike of ten pounds or less...

You can catch the odd really big fish on a small lure or bait (I have had a big pike on a single sprat) but generally speaking, as a rule of thumb - bigger lures attract bigger fish. In the same way that bigger baits attract bigger fish.

I started to experiment with 6 inch to 12 inch lures and found that the bigger (ten pound plus) or double figure pike became more interested... I know a pike fisherman who used an 'oversized' perch deadbait and was rewarded with a 24 pound pike! If you understand this and 'transition' to using bigger baits (such as mackerel) or bigger lures, you will be rewarded with (on average) bigger fish.

The big pike mentioned above didn't consider my ten gram

spinner worth his while but as soon as I put on a 'serious' lure he came out of the woodwork to attack it!

Twenty pound pike don't live on minnows and sticklebacks... You have to see it the way a big fish sees it... I know big plastic, wooden, or metal lures look big and 'clumsy' and the hooks tend to be big and obvious (to us) but to a fish it represents a meal worth chasing!

ONE OF MY BIGGEST LURE CAUGHT PIKE - AN "OTHERWORLDLY" MONSTER CAUGHT AT NIGHTFALL...

There is a big lake about half an hour away from where I live that I have been fishing for over twenty years. I have heard rumours of a really big pike being there. This lake has been there for decades and holds some really big carp, as well as specimen perch and huge chub. I have heard all sorts of rumours over the years - rumours of forty pound carp, rumours of a huge catfish, rumours of a monster pike...

I have heard all sorts. nobody knows what this lake really holds as it is a very big Lake and a bit of an unknown quantity. I have had spinners and plugs hit over the years by some very strong pike in this lake. One of which felt like a log... Now, this lake had come under a lot of fishing pressure from poachers and it was getting harder and harder to catch pike, every day, on account of these poachers knocking everything on the head and taking it home to eat. I gave it considerable thought and came to the conclusion that there had to be a lone survivor, one last "monster" in this lake, waiting to be caught by somebody who had the skill and the patience to do whatever it took to catch him. I decided to be that man... I would fish it relentlessly every day, until I caught the monster...

Every evening I made my way to the lake and back, regardless of the weather. It was summer time, somedays it was so hot that I was dripping with sweat before I got around the corner, on account of all the heavy gear that I was carrying. Some days I got soaked with rain. Some days there was thunder and lightning so I had to head home. Some days I caught one or two small Jacks. Some days I caught none. One day I caught a five pounder on a surface popper and began to wonder if that was all that there was left in this lake. I began to seriously have my doubts about any surviving monsters. Perhaps that era was over after all...

It seemed like I was flogging a dead horse - fishing the hardest water in the world. Perhaps, all that was left now was the Jacks... I carried on casting out and reeling in - mechanically now and in vain. Still, I carried on fishing until I had fished every peg on the lake several times over. I was just about to lose hope when one fruitless evening, I took my young apprentice (my nephew) fishing with me and I had to take him home for 9pm. I dropped him off at my sister's house and began the journey home on foot. On the way past the lake I had a compulsion to carry on fishing, even though it was half past nine at night and rapidly getting dark, not to mention a really spooky place to hang about late at night.

On account of darkness quickly falling, I decided to fish the nearest peg, a peg that I had previously had zero success on and usually bypassed in search of greener pastures. On this night, it would prove to be my good fortune. I put on a big (home made) surface popper and began to cast out as far as I could towards the nearest island - almost reaching it but falling slightly short every time. I was reeling in, in a slow, haphazard fashion and trying to create maximum noise, splashing and surface commotion, in order to imitate a frog or small mammal struggling to stay afloat on the surface. Visibility was low and I was rapidly running out of daylight.

All of a sudden, just as I was running out of line, a fish tried to grab my surface popper just as I was pulling it clear of the water ready to cast out again. The fish missed my lure but I had seen signs of a fish in my swim. Although there was nothing to suggest that it wasn't just another Jack. I cast my lure out a few more times but there were no follows, no takes, no tell tale bow waves or swirls - nothing.

I decided to change lures and carry on fishing even though it was about ten o clock at night now and completely dark. I decided to put on a Salmo replica lure that retailed at £10.99 but which I had bought for just £5.50 - half price out of the bargain bucket! It imitated a half pound carp. I cast out several times. Nothing. I carried on casting.

All of a sudden 'fish on' still there was no indication that this was a big fish. I half expected to bully in a small Jack. I strained my eyes to see what I had hooked in the darkness. I still couldn't see. Whatever it was, it felt heavy and it was definitely hooked. It started pulling back now, fighting harder, as I tried to pull it to the surface and towards the bank. "Oh wow" I said to myself, "this is the big one that I have been waiting for." Three times I pulled him towards the bank and tried to net him and three times he turned tail and shot off in the opposite direction towards the big island. On the fourth attempt, to my relief, I landed him, well her actually.

She was a solid fish - very, very solid, like an anaconda, a very muscular, heavy, solid fish, not like some of the big females that I have caught previously - soft bellied and full of eggs. This was a big, hard, heavy, muscular and well fed fish. She had a huge head and mouth and to put it bluntly looked quite capable of eating anything she liked! Her mouth was big enough to live on a diet of small carp or waterfowl. There was only one word to describe this fish. OTHERWORLDLY.

I unhooked her and stood back to admire my hard work which had finally paid off - at last. All the struggle, all the toil, all the effort, all the work. This fish had made it all worth while. It was 10.20pm at night when I landed this fish, in complete darkness and all alone. This was one of my proudest and best captures (at the time) but unfortunately I had no camera and no witnesses to see my triumph. One of my proudest captures on account of all the hard work, long hours and effort I had put in to catch it. For me this was definitely a 'trophy' fish. I released the big female, happy and elated that I had been the one fortunate enough to catch her but sad and disappointed that I had done so alone with no one to share the moment with. I was sad that I had to let the big, old girl go. So many hours of work for just a few short moments of pleasure and reward...

About two years or so later my fishing buddy caught the self same fish in a different peg on a floatfished perch. The float went under in broad daylight one evening and in less than half an hour. She fought hard once more.

That night, I learnt that...

SOMETIMES THERE IS A VERY THIN LINE BETWEEN SUCCESS AND FAILURE.

DOUBLE 'BLADE' SPINNERS

I don't rate double blade spinners as reliable fish catchers as I cannot recall ever catching a fish using this method or even getting a take for that matter!

To be honest, after 'blanking' one too many times I took all my double blade spinners apart and repurposed them by rebuilding them into regular, old fashioned single blade spinners! And unless you have had some success using them then I suggest that you do the same! I think that there is something a bit 'fishy' or phoney about two blade spinners and that is why in my experience fish avoid them. It seems strange to me that a single blade spinner is so successful but a double blader catches nothing! Perhaps, they just look too good to be true...

BALL BEARING FILLED PLASTIC LURES

My opinion on 'ball bearing' filled plastic lures is that they are unnatural, suspicious to fish, and useless. Generally   speaking the ball bearing or 'rattle' sound offers no real advantage. I have had such low success with these types of lures that I honestly believe that they have no or bare minimal value.

In my humble opinion: The rattle sound makes no difference to fish and contrary to the thinking behind them does not in fact attract fish! I have caught hundreds of fish on lures. To my knowledge, I have caught none on ball bearing rattle lures! Make of this what you will.

GOOD OLD FASHIONED PIKE SPOONS

These are good, reliable fish catchers and will catch pike (and specimen chub) everyday of the week! Believe it or not, again - most of my success has come from using home made 'table spoon' fishing spoons. I Just make them myself... I recommend nice big, bright, shiny ones. I have even had follows and takes on a 'shoe horn' spoon.

HOW TO MAKE YOUR OWN PIKE SPOONS...

Get yourself a nice, big, shiny table spoon... Drill a small hole in each end of the spoon. Then saw or snap off the spoon handle. Attach a large 'eye' and a rotating swivel at one end (for the wire trace to attach to) and attach an 'eye' and a large treble hook at the other end. Job done. You can attach some red wool to the hook shank if you like to make it more attractive/appealing to the pike...

HOW TO MAKE SPOON 'SPINNERS'

You can make a spoon 'spinner' in almost exactly the same way... You can use either a table spoon or a tea spoon for the 'blade' of the spinner. It doesn't matter which size. They both work - it's just personal preference. You can use any colour spoon you like... Silver or any other colour variation. Drill a small hole in one end (doesn't matter which) then saw or snap of the spoon handle. Get a large metal paperclip... Use pliers to bend/fashion a medium/large, round eye at one end (for the wire trace to attach to) then clip off any excess metal from the bend of the eye. Place the wire through the 'eye' of the spoon/spinner blade. Then place a single medium sized bead directly below or beneath the blade of the spinner. You can use a whole row of lightweight plastic beads all the way down to the hook or just one bead then a short length of clear or white plastic tube/tubing. The easiest place to find the plastic tubing is inside squirty handwash bottles/ spray bottle containers. Simply cut to exact size or 'length' with scissors. You can add a brightly coloured red/orange or any colour you like bead at the bottom of the length of plastic directly above the hook. Place the bottom end of the wire directly through the eye of a large treble hook or bend/fashion a medium/large 'eye' at the bottom. Clip off any excess wire then attach a lure 'eye' and a treble hook. The casting weight comes from the metal spoon itself. Hence why you can use lightweight tubular plastic/beads on the main 'body' of the spinner to hide/ disguise/decorate the length of wire. Oh, and these lures really do work just try one for your self... Pike love em and so do three, four, and five pound plus chub!

PIKE FLY IMITATION LURES...

These are not traditional pike fly's but lures with a long shank of metal wire surrounded with a piece of fabric or fur, a wire trace attachment eye at one end, and a treble hook at the other. They imitate a rat, mouse, water vole or small mammal. They are 4 to 6 inches long and gain their casting weight from water absorption. They are a slow sinking lure (if you stop reeling them in.) To be honest they are absolute dynamite lures. I have a red and white one which is mustard! I also have a nice black and white one.

The beauty of these lures is that you can easily make them yourself from an old teddy bear, a strip or two of fluffy cushion fabric or whatever. You can even add a wriggly tale... They glide through the water when you pull or retrieve them but the moment you stop pulling them they puff up like a puffer fish and sink down very slowly. These are a very worthwhile investment or lure making project. I highly recommend them!

You can catch pike on rat or water vole imitation lures (I have) If you can't find any to buy just make some yourself...

You can even catch pike on baby duckling imitation lures... Just use your imagination - the sky's the limit!

I am forever tampering with or altering lures. Snapping off dives, changing colours with paint or markers, adding hooks/removing hooks, changing hook sizes or just generally improving or modifying lures to suit my unique fishing needs.

Nothing is set in stone when it comes to fishing. Feel free to use your imagination and do things your own way. The very best anglers are inventors and innovators. Independent, freethinkers who push the boundaries/limits and experiment with new things all the time. That is what makes fishing such a fun and versatile sport.

Learn all the time - like a newborn baby. If you are not learning then you are not growing. If you are not growing, then you are not improving and if you are not improving all the time then how are you going to get any better?

IT IS BETTER TO 'REINVENT' THE WHEEL - THAN TO GET STUCK IN A RUT...

<u>LURE MAINTANENCE/PRESERVATION</u>

Always shake the water off your lures after using them and before putting them back in their boxes to prevent lures, eyelets and hooks going rusty.

Leave any used (wet) lures out to dry on the window sill or near a radiator when you get home to prevent your lures from rusting and rapidly deteriorating overnight.

<u>DISCARDING OLD USED HOOKS</u>

Always discard old, rusty, broken/snapped, blunt treble/hooks. You can easily snap individual sections of treble hook on super tough snags. Always replace the treble asap. I have lost fish on the take/strike due to having only two hooks on a treble hook that is supposed to hold three! The lure in question was a formidable spinner. I was reluctant to swap it, and instead lost a good fish instead by thinking that two hooks would suffice, it won't, (only as a last resort) you need three...

CHAPTER 10.
SPINNING FOR
CHUB AND TROUT

I have to be honest with you: Chub and trout will eat just about anything! I have even caught chub on big, horrible slimy slugs!

In regards to lure fishing or 'spinning' - some of the hardest and most memorable takes that I have ever had on lures have not come from pike. They have come from huge, specimen chub! I once caught a chub of about 5lbs or so on a big lake casting underneath a concrete bridge. I was lucky enough to witness this big brute appear out of nowhere and take a 10g silver spinner on a rainy, wet day when the water was the colour of clay. And let me say that this fish was a true predator and operating on pure killer instinct. He didn't just nail my spinner. No sir, he absolutely hammered it. Bang, gone, just like that.

MUDDY WATER CHUB ON SPINNERS

The lake where I was fishing is full of pike but when the water is heavily coloured you can hardly catch one and I do mean that it is near enough impossible. I fished this particular lake for ten years without ever catching a chub. Until we had lots of rain and I got fed up of waiting for the weather to improve and decided to go fishing 'whatever the weather.' I caught a 3 pound plus chub on a spinner in brown muddy water! This came as a surprise to me as I had never caught a chub on a lure in that lake even though I knew that there are some humdingers in there. As a matter of fact, I had never heard of anyone catching a chub on a lure in that lake. I went on to catch at least three big chub that day on spinners. I have never caught a chub of less than about three pounds on that water due to the presence of large pike.

Since then, it is quite common for me now, to go spinning in rainy and poor conditions (when the pike are not feeding) and expect to catch a handful of big chub when I would otherwise not be able to catch anything. I put this down to one or all of three possible things.

1. The chub hunt more confidently and efficiently due to the heavily discoloured water serving to hide or camouflage them on the hunt.

2. The chub know instinctively or have learnt through observation and/or experience that the pike dislike muddy/cloudy water and being primarily a sight feeder prefer to feed in clear water thus muddy/cloudy/discoloured water represents relative safety and freedom for the chub to prowl about, roam and hunt in peace and safety. The chub know that the pike represent little or no threat to them. I thoroughly believe this because I have seriously struggled to catch pike at all on lures in heavily discoloured water and yet the ordinarily shy, cautious chub seem to throw caution to the wind and go on the rampage. Even when I have seen pike near the bank they have always been facing the bank not the water and their body language suggests that they are neither hunting nor feeding.

3. The chub cannot find food to eat as easily due to the water discolouration and so go for much more obvious targets such as bright silver or gold spinners!

Another time, way back in the summer of 2000. I was trying out a new water for pike. I cast out a big (silver, red and black) ondex spinner and got one of the hardest takes ever... I thought I was into a big pike... Imagine my surprise when reluctantly and after giving a great account of itself in comes a huge chub! I caught another two big chub on surface poppers on the same outing. It turned out that there were no pike present in this water. There were predators present though! I caught plenty more big chub on spinners and surface poppers. It did not come as a surprise to me that chub are predators or that you could catch chub on lures (I have known and experienced this from being a teenager.) What came as a surprise was just how HARD chub hit lures!

I have caught chub on surface popping lures (they can hardly resist them) and indeed I no sooner reel one in and release it than another chub takes exactly the same lure in exactly the same swim. My friend once caught a big chub on a homemade spinner - made using a table spoon as the spinning blade (a table spoon spinner - not a table spoon - spoon). After catching a big chub He turned to me and said "I didn't half feel that take." This same friend who I started fishing with almost 20 years ago and sometimes fish with once or twice a week has also caught a chub of about 5 pounds or so on a perch imitation lure in a midlands canal. A local man who fishes the canal regularly says that you cannot run a lure through it without huge chub nailing your lures. In fact, he says that the chub home in on your lures before the pike do!

GREEDY OPPORTUNISTIC TROUT

Trout are wild, beautiful, and graceful creatures. Brown, common and rainbow trout are all great sport and a very hard fighting and acrobatic species of fish.

Trout are an aggressive, territorial species of fish. They are predators in their own right. They do not only eat flies and insects as some people think. Like chub and carp - they are opportunist hunters and feeders who will take advantage of any and every potential food source in their environment. I have seen a trout jump clear out of the water and take a moth right out of the air! They can easily be caught on swimfeedered maggots or freelined worms. They will eat bread, and fish and chips that is thrown in to them. I have even caught and gutted trout with bellies full of fish and chips! I have caught a trout with a belly stuffed with sweetcorn. I once caught a trout with a great, big, spicy fried chicken bone in its belly about the size of a large human thumb! That and two lengths of soft white silicone such as you get around your windows, sink, or bath. I have caught trout two feet long and about 3 pounds plus in weight with bellies filled with nothing but freshwater snails. In one case 32 snails and a small pebble the size of a thumb nail.

I once peered under a bridge and saw a wild trout eating silk weed that had floated downstream. As a child, I once caught a trout in a net, in a small stream, and upon examining him in a bucket he spat out a bullhead! A short while ago, I spoke to a man, who told me, he float fished a bullhead as live bait, on a small river, and caught a 2 and a half pound brown trout! I have caught trout with sticklebacks in their stomachs. I have caught a trout on a brown, plastic, trout imitation pike plug with a perch hanging out of the back of its throat and another four or five perch in his belly and this on more than one occasion. Trout are greedy, opportunistic, cannibalistic, predatory hunters and feeders. Like carp and chub, they can be caught on just about anything!

<u>A GRUESOME DISCOVERY</u>

A few years ago, I was fishing a small, local river. As is my custom of old... I cast out a freelined lobworm into the dark gloomy water and watched it drift into the darkness underneath a bridge/tunnel. Trout like bridges and tunnels you know! After a few minutes, I felt a pull on my line so I struck instantly. I had hooked something quite some distance away and I could hear it breaking the surface and splashing about underneath this bridge/tunnel. I reeled in to discover that it was a trout of about two feet in length and about two pounds in weight. I decided to take it home for the mrs. When I got this trout home, I observed it more carefully in the kitchen sink. I noticed that it had a rock hard lump in its belly! It was about the size of a large bullhead, but felt too hard to be a fish... "I wonder what on earth that is?" I thought to myself...

As I gutted the trout, this is what I found: Two small water snails, two pieces of sweetcorn, two long pieces of white silicone! (like you get around your bath.) Don't ask... And the remains of a four inch KFC style 'spicy' chicken drumstick bone! I don't know how the trout managed to swallow it without choking itself! Needless to say, when I showed the mrs she was not impressed and not so keen on eating the trout anymore... "Urghh, that's disgusting!" she said (It was gross) but she wasn't put off by it being caught on a great, big, slimy lobworm! "Aren't you going to eat it now then?" I asked. "No chance, not now I've seen that" she said. "What am I supposed to do with it now then?" I asked her. "I don't care but I'm not eating it!" she replied. "No worries then, I'll give it to the mother in law!" I said, "but what about the big bone in it's belly?" The mrs asked. "He, he, he - she'll never know" I said with a chuckle...

BLACK JACK

When I was a school kid, I used to fish, for hours on end, under a bridge/tunnel, for common and wild brown trout, using mixed maggots or worms for bait. I caught the odd trout but nothing that special. What kept me going back there, day after day, and time after time, during the cold winter months was black jack...

Black jack was the story, no - the myth of a huge brown trout nicknamed black jack that everybody was trying to catch, which was handed down to me through the grapevine. I spent many hours on my own trying to catch black jack one winter. I never succeeded. I don't know whether somebody else caught black jack and ate him or if indeed black jack ever existed. All I know is: I never saw him or caught him, but by all accounts he was a very wise, wily old fish...

Fast forward about 20 years...

THE REAL BLACK JACK

When I was in my early thirties I started spinning for big common, and wild brown trout in a small local river. I caught a fair few common and brown trout averaging about twenty four inches in length (two feet) and two or three pounds in weight. One of my course fisherman friends caught a twenty six inch long (2 ft 2 inch) common trout weighing 3.7 lb's on a worm, in a spot I showed him. I knew the fish was there but wanted to help him catch it, as he had never caught a trout before. Another good friend of mine caught a big, brown trout on floating bread in the same river which reportedly weighed 4.5 lbs.

There was one brown trout in particular that I wanted to catch. He was a wise and wily, battle scarred, old brown trout. I named him black jack! (on account of his very unusual colouring.) Blackjack was the darkest trout that I had ever seen. Not a brown trout, but a black one! and big too. I had a six inch, blue, pike lure (Abu Garcia Tormentor) which he chased, and attacked, on one occasion, in this same river when I was targeting pike. He was very dark on account of him living and swimming in deep, dark, muddy stretches of river. Nobody knew he was there. He was also exceptionally hard to catch on account of him moving up and down river a lot and never being seen in the same stretch twice. I only tried for him on artificial lures (usually home made spinners) and never used bread, worms or maggots on account of the sporting aspect of fishing. I thought he was a special fish and I wanted to catch him in my own way.

It took me three years to catch him but I eventually did and on one of my own homemade, trademark spinners none the less. My friend had just pulled out a nice jack pike and I hooked blackjack on the very next cast of my spinner in the same swim. It took me completely by surprise. This fish was so black, old, bruised and battered looking that it looked like a fish called a burbot that is or was almost completely extinct in the british isles. I knew it couldn't be a burbot on account of their rarity but that is what it looked like in the water and when I pulled my hook out of its huge mouth! You could really tell that this was a wisened, battle-scarred old fish that did not take kindly to me catching it one bit! But catch it I did - eventually!

The bummer is that the fish kicked when my friend was about to take a photograph of it for me and so I accidently dropped it back into the water before having a chance to photograph it! No matter, I may catch it again one day if I'm lucky! I have caught bigger trout (fresh water and sea trout) but I have never caught a trout that dark, before or since and the amazing thing is - that these trout survive at all, in pike infested rivers like these.

A VERY SUCCESSFUL DAYS TROUT FISHING...

One glorious day a few summers ago, for whatever reason I hit the jackpot trout fishing on the Derwent. I don't know if it was right place, right time or every dog has his day or what, but It seemed as if every trout in the river was in my swim! I caught a fish almost every single cast. Sometimes six fish followed my spinner back to the bank. It seemed I could do no wrong. Every cast was a winner and everything I touched that day turned to gold I lost count of the number of trout I caught spinning that day but it was a lot! I honestly believe that had I had a full days sport instead of just a few short hours then I may have caught over a hundred fish!

SPINNING FOR TROUT

Spinning for trout is a piece of cake. It is always best when river fishing to cast diagonally towards the opposite bank to the one that you are fishing on. Cast out as far as you can without overcasting on to the opposite bank. Expect to get instant takes 'on the drop' and always reel in as slowly as you can without hitting the bottom and getting snagged. You can catch trout spinning on the surface of the water (with mackerel spinners) and spinning down deep on the bottom of the water. Trout hunt and feed actively at all depths. In summer, may/june time when the mayflies are out it is usually best to spin in the top section of the water as trout are actively feeding off the top on mayflies and other insects. In the colder months you are probably better off spinning deeper. You can catch trout successfully by casting and spinning both up and down stream. When your swim goes quiet, move on to the next peg/swim. Don't waste time fishing when the fish have switched off/moved on. If you know that the fish are still there but they are not responding to your spinners/lures then sometimes it is worth changing spinners/lures as this can fool the trout and start getting you takes again.

You can successfully stalk trout by deliberately casting to the location of rises last seen on the surface of the water. Cast to the rise or past it and be ready to strike. When spinning for trout you need to have fast reflexes on the strike and a stiff action rod, otherwise you will miss/lose a lot of takes. One thing I have noticed though is that you hook more fish when you have got cotton or feathers on your spinner hook. Blue spinner blades work well. As do black blades and red, black, blue and yellow feathers on the hook but don't overthink it as trout are very curious, instinctive, aggressive, predatory and territorial fish.

You need to scale down the size of your spinners, spinner blades and hooks. 6 - 10 gram spinners are plenty big enough and size 6 treble hooks are about as big as you would ever need to go. Be open minded and experiment. *Success begets assurance.*

MY BIGGEST RAINBOW TROUT...

I mentioned at the beginning of this book catching an 'enormous' rainbow trout and being 'spoiled for life' by the experience. I was not joking, as I am about to relay...

I was spinning on the river Derwent... (Which is classed as one of the top three chalk streams in the world) I cast out as far as I could downstream and my spinner landed perfectly for the 'umpteenth' time right on the edge of the opposite bank, directly below the over-hanging branches of an old willow tree... I knew that it was deep water there, so I reeled in as slowly as I could... Letting the strong current of the river and the blade of my home-made spinner do all the work...

As the lure slowly descended into the depths...

All of a sudden, I instantly felt a huge weight on the end of my line. I struck hard and began to reel in... I didn't know it at the time but this was the biggest (rainbow) trout that I had ever hooked! It felt like a lead weight! As it approached the bank it seemed to get bigger and bigger!

The strange thing was that unlike the countless other common, brown, and rainbow trout that I have caught in the past... This one fought completely differently. There were no airborne gymnastics or 'acrobatics.'

The huge fish simply bent one way, and then the other, one way and then the other, over and over again, in a kind of seemingly 'slow motion' completely 'predictable' fashion. She was simply too big, fat and wide to do any other!

Anyone who has ever caught a fish like this will know exactly what I am talking about. The size and weight of the fish combined with the river Derwent's strong current made it a bit of a struggle to land the fish but land her I did - eventually. I knew what was at stake, I knew this was a personal best fish! It was a bit of a boring, predictable fight in a way but the fish did fight and she fought hard - almost too hard!

REST, RECOVERY AND SAFE RETURN...

The point of the story is this: By the time I landed that big trout she was absolutely knackered (exhausted) and needed to get her breath back - badly! If it had of been a human being they would have been put on oxygen! I had to let the fish catch its breath and fully recover...

I had no intention of taking the fish home for the mrs (for the dinner table.) The fish was simply "too big" and it would have been a waste of a 'trophy' fish. I wanted the fish to "live to fight another day!" She was too good a fish to die needlessly on the bank...

I wanted her to make a full recovery so that somebody else could catch her again some day!

As an experienced fisherman: I recognised that the fish was extremely fatigued and needed to be handled with great care in order to make a full and complete recovery...

I quickly unhooked her and placed her carefully back in the water. I held her in my hands very gently. I made sure that she was facing upstream (to make it easier for her to breathe.) I placed her in the shallows, in some slack water where the current was less strong. She lay alongside a log and took about ten minutes to fully recover before slowly swimming away...

I am proud of the way I handled that fish that day. I am under no illusions that some fish are quite capable of fighting themselves to the point of exhaustion and beyond...

I am very confident that my 'trophy' fish lived to fight another day... Which in the end, is all that mattered.

The moral of the story is this: Sometimes you have to have your "finger on the pulse" and learn to recognise and 'realise' just how much a "hard battle" can take out of a big fish...

You have to bear in mind that the fish "fought as hard as it could" but all to no avail...

Proper fish care decides and dictates the ultimate fate of the captured fish. With 'proper care and treatment' they can go on to "live to fight another day." Without due care and consideration it could very well be a trophy fish's 'last battle.' Ultimately, the fish's welfare is what really matters...

CHAPTER 11. USING LIVE, DEAD & 'MICRO' BAITS...

<u>USING 'SEA FISH' DEADBAITS</u>

Dead baiting has accounted for captures of some literally huge fish. My younger brother loves it, he has captured twenty odd pound pike. Last I heard his biggest pike was twenty four pounds, his mate got one of thirty two! My brother likes to use lamprey, perch and mackerel for bait. Roach, perch, trout and pike make good dead baits. Do not be hesitant to use baits of the sea fishing variety as experience has taught me that (oddly) they work just as well for catching pike and catfish.

Of the sea fishing variety: I like mackerel, sprats, sardines, herrings and smelts (in that order.) As I just mentioned in the previous chapter: I once caught a 5 foot long, 40 pound plus catfish (whilst night-fishing) on half a herring...

Do not be put off by the relatively small size of sprats... They are great baits (super smelly.) I have accounted for some big pike using sprats and (surprisingly) I have had a couple of big perch using a single sprat for bait. Mackerel are a great (smelly) bait. They have a nice pattern - a bit like a jack pike... They work really well for targeting pike of the larger variety. Do not be put off by their large size. Cut them in half if you think a full one is 'too big.' Mackerel and sprats are my all time favourite sea fish dead baits.

A BIG PIKE AND A 'HEADLESS' SPRAT...

A few miles from where I live, there is a lovely little river, that I have been fishing for many years. A quiet place that is very close to my heart, it runs for several miles largely unnoticed through a small town centre. One cold, chilly, winter's day about fourteen years ago, whilst slowly walking along the edge of the river, carefully observing the water (as is my custom of old.) I had seen an impressive pike lurking around near the bank. I decided to go and fish this nice, slow flowing, deep bend.

It was a nice intimate spot on a corner where the slow flowing river takes a right turn, there was plenty of weed cover and shade and it looked very promising. I quickly set up my one piece six foot rod and attached a length of dark green leader. I put on one size six treble hook and used a wine bottle cork for a float! I set the depth between my hook and my float at about four or so feet deep, hooked a shiny, silver sprat right behind the head, and flicked it out gently into the flow in front of me...

A little time went by as it does, I don't really notice these things as time always stands still for me when I am fishing... But my then girlfriend (who is now my wife) was stood next to me shivering, telling me how bored she was, and moaning about how cold it was...

I took no notice of her. There I stood, a fully grown man, fascinated by a little wooden cork bobbing it's way along downstream... I stood there perfectly still, completely focused, fixated even, on that all important piece of driftwood... My float was acting very suspiciously and anything she said at that moment was of no interest to me. At the exact moment my float went under... She blurted out "I'm going home." "Just wait one moment" I replied. "No, It's cold, I've had enough now, and I'm going home!" She stormed off. My float was steaming away to my right as she stormed off to my left. I struck, "I've got a fish on!" I shouted. "Course you have!" she shouted back. I couldn't believe it, the silly woman didn't believe me! She honestly thought I was trying to trick her into hanging around with the 'empty promise' of a fish! A fish! My mrs doesn't even care about fish! She doesn't even like fish!

I didn't have time to argue. I began to put some pressure on this fish that was taking off on a furious run... My rod was bending into it nicely... For just a second, I glanced over my left shoulder at the mrs storming off and then back to the spot where my line entered the water. All of a sudden - tug, tug and then nothing. The fish was off. I was gutted. I reeled in my line to find that all I had left on my hook was a sprats head! "That's her fault for distracting me" I said to myself. I looked over my left shoulder, she was long gone. No doubt she thought I was going to come running after her... "fat chance" I muttered to myself. I had bigger fish to fry.

I put on another, nice, shiny sprat and looked all around my swim. "Now, where is that big pike?" I said to myself. I walked down stream but I couldn't see any signs of it anywhere. I crossed a bridge a couple of pegs down and began to stealthily sneak back up river, hoping to sneak up on that big, hungry, elusive pike. I found a spot roughly opposite to where I had lost the big pike. The water was crystal clear. I tossed my sprat into the water and crouched perfectly still near a small tree to my left. My sprat fluttered enticingly down to the bottom of the river bed.

As I watched my sprat work it's magic, all of a sudden - there she was - slightly to my left, hovering menacingly at mid-depth. I stayed perfectly still, The pike didn't seem to know I was there. She was a beautiful specimen, perfectly proportioned - long, dark green and fat. She was mesmerised by my little sprat and had complete 'tunnel vision.' As did I.

I had caught her completely unawares... She looked down her mean, ugly snout at my pathetic, little sprat which now seemed tiny and almost insignificant. She nose-dived to take my sprat... Her snout reached the river bed and simultaneously her huge red tail almost came completely out of the water. "Bingo" I thought to myself. She snaffled my sprat. "One, two, three" I counted "strike!" The big pike started going nuts... Her gills flaring and her huge head and tail, thrashing left and right furiously. Every time she opened that huge, cavernous mouth I held my breath in anticipation as I was sure my little sprat and single treble hook was going to come flying out of that huge mouth... (again) but as luck would have it - my hook hold held this time... Being hooked at such close range I saw the entire fight unfold right in front of my eyes...

The big pike fought and struggled ferociously, like an angry crocodile, desperate to shake off my little size six treble. Her big mouth opening wide for a few seconds at a time and then closing again, threatening to throw off my little, lone hook at any second. I played her as best I could on a six foot rod and at close range, careful to keep tension on the line the whole time and put plenty of pressure on the pike. After a few minutes of heart racing excitement she tired out, came up to the surface and rolled onto her side. It was a very welcome sight. I was relieved and elated at the same time. At last, there she lay - almost within my grasp, now if I could just get my hands on her...

I creeped carefully down the slippery grass bank and hung precariously over the waters edge as I chinned the huge pike. I heaved her up and lay her down carefully on the bank in front of me. She was a beauty, a fine specimen of a pike. As I recall, she had a big, soft, fat belly, a very large 'monstrous' head, eyeballs like a sheep, and a huge cavernous mouth, with some very serious hardware inside - a real toothy critter! Needless to say I knew the mrs would never believe me! A week or two later I went back to the self same spot and caught another big pike in the same swim, using the exact same method, and the second pike was 'almost' as big as the first one.

TRAVEL LIGHT IT'S MORE FUN...

That first day I had gone fishing with almost no gear. I mean the absolute bare minimal essentials. I tend to find those light travelling days the most enjoyable, the most fun and rewarding... They force me to do what I had to do as a youngster... Namely rely on my own ingenuity, creativity and resourcefulness, instead of a back breaking amount of tackle!

COARSE FISH DEADBAITS

There is a popular saying: 'A fish smells from the head.' With that being said I prefer to use the tail section! I like to cut them in half at a nice, neat angle (to make them easier for the fish to eat.) I also like to slide a tie wrap through the eye of the treble hook and pull it tight on the base or 'root' of the fish's tail fin. This is a little trick I learned to stop myself losing baits on the cast... My piking buddy prefers to use the head so we make a good team! I do this with mackerel tails, whole sprats, roach, perch, chub, trout and other deadbaits of the sea fish variety.

Generally speaking, all or most dead baits work well as pike/catfish are opportunist scavengers who are able to use their strong sense of smell to locate food. That being said, pike are primarily sight feeders so a nice, bright, shiny, silver bait is always going to appeal. Roach, perch, chub, trout and gudgeon all make excellent deadbaits...

Unlike my brother who is a big fan of using lamprey for deadbait, I have never had any success using lamprey for bait. I prefer to use roach, perch or chub. Just saying. But it may just be down to what the fish are 'used to' eating. Where there are many trout I am sure that rainbow, brown and common trout make the best baits. Lamprey are just unpleasant in general, especially the live ones - horrible slimy, wriggly, parasitic, blood sucking things. Ughh! I've caught a fair few of them whilst landnetting for bullheads. I don't like them. I think that technically they are classed as 'eels' but they are more like a parasitic worm than a fish to me. They have gills but they are just gross!

WIRELEADERS

A longer wire leader is very much preferable to a shorter one for catching big pike. A 6 - 8 inch wire leader is okay for catching small jack (male) pike. However, I would recommend a 12 - 18 inch wire leader when fishing for big pike or when fishing somewhere where an unexpected large female pike could turn up out of the blue. A pike has a disproportionately large head and mouth in relation to its body. As a rough guide: I would say that a pike's head and thus mouth represents about one third of its total body length! pike can realistically grow to over 4ft in length! Although you may never encounter a pike that measures over 4ft in length (never say never.) The chances are that you will sooner or later encounter a pike that measures 3ft or more in length. I have encountered many such fish. A pike of this size will undoubtably have a head of 12 - 15 inches long or a good foot plus. It will also undoubtably have a very large, cavernous mouth for engulfing it's prey. When you consider that all pike are long, missile shaped, streamlined predators with disproportionately large heads and cavernous mouths (compared to other fish) you will soon see that a 6 - 8 inch wire leader is woefully inadequate. Do not make the mistake of losing the fish of a lifetime all for the sake of overlooking one very important detail. If you only have short wire leaders - then double them up! Or else make some long ones up at home. Remember: Preparation and organisation are the keys to your success.

A GOOD FISHERMAN DOES HIS PREPARATION AT HOME - THE DAY BEFORE.

A BAD FISHERMAN DOES HIS PREPARATION AT THE WATERS EDGE...

If you are a beginner or novice and are having any doubts about a pike's ability to shear through line then let me assure you that a pike's teeth can shear through strong line (18lb mono or 30lb braid) with the greatest of ease. If you are an experienced pike fisherman and have seen the pike's toothy 'hardware' the gill flaring and head thrashing of a large pike, then you will know exactly what I am talking about.

Double up your wire leaders... Long wire traces (12 - 18 inches in length) tend to end up all twisted and 'frazzled' after a while. The simplest solution is to use two or even three shorter (6 - 8 inches each) wire leaders clipped together. This is what I do and it solves the problem quite easily. Remember - the longer the wire leader the better!

<u>WIRE LEADER/TRACE COLOUR PREFERENCES...</u>

I like to use a silver coloured wire leader in clear water.

A green coloured wire leader in green water.

And a black wire leader in dark, rainy, muddy or discoloured water.

The choice is yours...

<u>TEMPORARILY RESTORING WIRE LEADERS</u>

If you are lure fishing and one of you're wire leaders becomes 'frazzled' - i.e. kinked or twisted, attach it to your jacket zipper at one end and hold it straight and tight at the other end. Then take out a lighter and run it slowly but steadily up and down the length of the wire leader. Be careful to keep the wire in the centre of the blue flame (where the flame is hottest.) After 2 or 3 'runs' blow on the wire leader. The wire leader should now be either completely straight or significantly straighter and more manageable/useable than it was previously.

Please note: This method will melt the plastic on plastic coated wire leaders but will straighten them out nonetheless.

This method could also potentially weaken the overall strength or breaking strain of the wire leader but is still useful (as a very last resort.)

<u>USING WIRE TRACES OR 'LEADERS'</u>

Always use a wire trace, preferably a long one of twelve to eighteen inches in length. Or two shorter six - eight inch traces clipped together or 'doubled' up. This is not so important if you are targeting catfish and there are no pike present but be aware that even catfish have abrasive pads in their mouths. I recommend using two large - size six or size four trebles (spaced about four inches apart) when targeting pike and either two large (size four) trebles or a single large sea fishing hook or rig when targeting catfish. Just remember that pike and catfish have large, hard mouths so you will need big 'sharp' hooks to catch them. Also, a catfish's mouth is so big that you can actually accidently pull the bait out of the fish's mouth on the strike, if your hooks don't find a home and penetrate.

ELIMINATING MISTAKES

<u>SNAP OFFS</u>

A snap off can be caused by one of several things:

1. Weak or old/poor quality, cheap line, line faults - always check for these. Line faults can be caused by the clip on your reel spool, a hard snag overstretching, straining or weakening your line, getting your line caught in trees, brambles or thornbushes, abrasion caused by (scratched or damaged) plastic rod rings or worse sharp plastic on broken rod rings caused by dropping or mishandling your rod (I am guilty of this one.) Or even a freak knot or unexplainable fault in your line. This list is not exhaustive.

2. A bad knot - there is really no excuse for this as it takes ten seconds to tie a good, solid knot. The Grinner knot (an oldie

but a goodie) is truly a remarkable knot that you can put 100% confidence in. It will NEVER let you down. Nowadays I ALWAYS use the four or preferably five turn grinner knot. I use it for tying line to my reel spools as well as for tying on hooks, wire traces, swivels, line to line and everything else. I cannot recommend this knot highly enough, it is simply the best.

3. Incorrectly set drag - if your drag is set too tight it will fail to give line at the critical moment. Most anglers know how to set their drags correctly. What sometimes catches people out (especially when lure fishing) is when they get snagged. They then (rightly) tighten their drag right up in order to free their lure/hooks. After freeing up their hooks, they reel in, inspect their bait/lure and cast out again - forgetting to re-adjust their drag. It is surprising how often this happens. I have done it, you have done it, we have all done it!

4. Using a wire trace or leader that is too short! This is a real schoolboy error. Like I have said before a six to eight inch leader is fine for catching jacks but how do you know that 'big mama' isn't going to appear out of nowhere and snatch your lure? Answer - you don't! I used to think that an eighteen inch wire leader sounded too long - excessive even. I thought a twelve inch leader would suffice! How wrong I was... What changed my mind was when I caught a pike of about seventeen pounds and upon landing him I noticed that my line was literally an inch or two from the tip of his nose! This was far too close for comfort. I thought I might be snapped off at any given moment. I figured any sudden turn or head movement might sever my line. I well and truly learned my lesson that day! In my opinion the longer the wire trace - the better! If in doubt - double up. Better to be safe than sorry.

CIRCLE HOOKS...

Circle hooks are a great invention. The advantage of using a 'circle' hook is that you don't have to 'strike.' You can simply reel in (slowly) and 'tighten up' on the fish and the sharp point of the hook will still penetrate the fish's mouth. I have had a very high (maybe 100 percent) success hook rate using circle hooks so I would definitely recommend using them... (You don't tend to lose fish on them.)

TIMING YOUR STRIKE

Pike and catfish are greedy, sometimes a big one can gorge itself on your bait very quickly, if you hesitate too long they can get 'deep hooked.' Strike too soon and you could pull the bait right out of the fish's mouth. Strike too late and you could end up with a deep hooked fish. It all depends on the size of your bait in relation to the size of the fish. Again, pike and catfish have big mouths and can make quick work of your bait. If you are using a small, soft bait such as a sprat then I recommend striking quickly - there is no need to hesitate. If you are using a larger bait such as half a mackerel then perhaps take your time and play it by ear. Sometimes, I like to strike straight away (as you would when lure fishing) as this eliminates the possibility of deep hooking fish. I do not recommend using very large or heavy baits for pike as when the pike does his tell tale, trademark gill flare and head thrash combo in an attempt to throw off the hooks - the weight of a big bait can play into the pikes hands and make it possible and indeed more likely for the pike to successfully throw the hooks. You heard it here first.

Using live or dead baits generally falls into one of two categories...

FLOAT FISHED LIVE/DEAD BAITS

For those who are older, less active, or mobile - walking miles all day whilst carrying a rod and a heavy bag full of lures/gear may not seem like a very exciting prospect or a very realistic option. Whilst sitting down and relaxing behind a live or dead bait may be...

The rules/laws on livebaiting are constantly changing and different all over the world so you will have to check them out for yourself depending on what country you live in and where you are planning to fish...

I like to use a homemade wine bottle cork float or a 15 - 20 gram clear plastic/bubble float as I think that the presentation is more natural/subtle. A plastic bubble float can be half filled with water to give more casting weight when using light baits such as sprats. This allows you to cast out further and thus get the bait exactly where you want it which is half the battle. I do think that big pike can become 'wise' to bright orange tipped pike floats when there is considerable fishing 'pressure'. A big wine bottle cork is so bouyant that it will hold up half a mackerel. I like to use a quick release clip attached to my wine bottle cork by wire from a paper clip, a couple of green pieces of elastic bands and a good old granny knot to secure the depth of the float. When the water is dark or murky it is probably best to fish your baits on or just off the bottom. When the water is crystal clear or there is reasonably good visibility you can fish your baits two - four feet beneath the surface and a pike will still see it and come up to the top to take it even in very deep (twelve feet) water. This is due to the pike's binocular vision as they primarily see what is in front of them and above them in the water. This helps with avoiding predatory birds and hunting small mammals such as water voles/shrews, rats, frogs, toads and small water birds such as coots, ducklings and moorhens. I like to double up (link) my wire traces together to prevent kinkage or a frazzled/bent/ twisted wire trace. When it comes to rigs I think there is nothing better than simplicity itself. Don't put anything on your line that does not need to be on your line. I'm a big believer in natural presentation or as close to it as you can get. That's why I highly rate and recommend 'freelining' whenever you can. freelining is simply having nothing else on your line than a hook and some bait. Obviously, when float fishing for pike you have got to have a float, a wire trace, hook/s and bait. In my opinion anything more than this is usually just overthinking things. Things like: three way swivels and ledger bombs are just overcomplicating what is a very simple pastime. I have no use for them. What you need is convenience and simplicity, not 'sophistication.'

USING TIE WRAPS FOR ADDED SECURITY

There is however, one essential item that I would never be without - tie wraps! I like to thread a very small white or black tie wrap around the root of the tail fin, and feed it back through the eye of the treble hook, then pull it tight, and clip it off with a small pair of scissors or nail clips, thus ensuring that your bait NEVER comes flying off the hook when casting out and allowing you to fish with complete confidence and cast out as far and as hard as you like without the fear of losing your bait. This prevents losing deadbaits on the cast. Which you do not ever want to be doing as it gives pike or catfish an alternative 'free' food offering which they are just as likely to take as the one on your hook. If you make this schoolboy error then you are thus fishing against yourself and could miss out on the fish of a lifetime.

One time years ago, I was attempting a very ambitious, long, tricky cast (past an overhanging tree) out towards the very edge of an island. With a lot of effort, I cast out a dead roach (which flew off the hooks) and landed in exactly the place where I wanted it to. It then fluttered down enticingly and I watched in horror as a pike came out and grabbed it! Sadly, my hooks were not attached and it was my last deadait of the day!

Nowadays, I always secure my deadbaits via the tail root with tie wraps! Another thing to bear in mind is that pike and catfish swallow baits head first so you have to make sure your hook points are facing the correct way (towards your bait's tail) so as to set your hooks properly on the strike. Also, bear in mind that hooks move/adjust and slip so you have to check them in between casts to make sure that they are STILL facing the correct way. Otherwise, all is in vain. Always match your tie wraps with the colour of your baits... Use white or clear tie wraps for 'silvery' coloured fish and black ones for perch (they blend in with the stripes.)

A GOOD ANGLER ALWAYS ELIMINATES UNNECESSARY MISTAKES...

BOTTOM FISHED/FREELINED/LEDGERED DEAD BAITS

In my opinion, fishing dead baits 'on the bottom' is the most 'natural' presentation...

I like to freeline dead baits on the bottom, no weights, no leads, just a bait, hook/s wire trace/s and preferably a set baitrunner/ rear drag system or a set bite alarm. You cannot beat simplicity. I have got no time for overly complicated rigs.

In my opinion, the perfect rig is a simple one that can be put together in seconds with minimum time and fuss. As I have said before: You cannot beat half a mackerel, a nice sprat, or whatever 'natural' coarse fish the pike are eating on a daily basis. I highly recommend roach, perch, trout and pike. As above - don't forget to use tie wraps to lock your bait onto your hook. One tie wrap fed through the eye of the treble hook and wrapped around the tail root of a mackerel, sprat, perch, trout or whatever (with the excess tie wrap clipped off) takes seconds and makes all the difference in the world. Especially when you are using soft bodied baits like roach, mackerel, sardines,or sprats. With these baits and other soft bodied fish the hooks can easily pull loose on the cast. Not good if it was your last piece of bait! Just remember to match the tie wrap colour with the bait fish! So it blends in, instead of standing out...

SINK AND DRAW - SPINNING OR WOBBLING DEADBAITS

Spinning or wobbling deadbaits is a lost art - a forgotten, neglected element of pike fishing. It used to be very popular in the olden days - when lures were expensive, less life like, and hard to come by. The pike fishermen of previous generations used this method and indeed relied on it. It was their secret weapon. They knew something that modern fishermen don't seem to realise...

SINK AND DRAW, SPINNING, OR 'WOBBLING' DEADBAIT'S IS AN ABSOLUTELY DEVASTATING METHOD OF CATCHING BIG FISH...

Your author knows this. I studied the methods of the ancients, the 'masters.' There are no flies on me. The fact that this is a forgotten/neglected method of fishing and has slipped into the history books or 'obscurity' is one hundred percent to your advantage. The best fish to use is a small perch, chub or pike but if you cannot find one of these then buy some sprats from the supermarket. Use a small fish, no bigger than six inches but preferably four or five inches in length. Perch are ideal because they are very hardy and, one perch, set up on the correct rig should last you all day long - even if you catch several big pike. Likewise, chub and small pike are also ideal for the same reason because they are tough and hardy fish. Create a secure rig and simply cast it out as you would a lure. Then simply twitch or wobble the fish back in until you feel some resistance on the end of your line. When you feel a dead weight on the end of your line then strike immediately and HARD. Boom - you're in business! It's that easy! Striking on a sink and draw rig or when 'wobbling' deadbaits is exactly the same as when using a lure... You should strike with full conviction, there should be absolutely no hesitation whatsoever. The best freshwater fish for sink and draw/wobbling... Are perch, pike, chub, trout and roach...

SINK AND DRAW/WOBBLING TECHNIQUE...

I favour using a very simple, traditional, old fashioned technique as follows: Cast out, let your bait drop through the water column at an estimated rate of 1 second per foot until you reach your desired depth. Then quickly twitch your rod tip (kind of like a mini 'half hearted' strike.) Then reel in the slack line... A little twitch should only need one revolution or 'turn' of the reel handle. A slightly bigger twitch may require two, and three, and four, and so on. Just vary the rod tip pulls and revolutions of the reel handle between one and four revolutions/turns. Use your imagination... Make it haphazard, 'erratic' and unpredictable... You can repeatedly lift the bait up to the top of the water and let it drift/flutter back down (enticingly) over and over again until you get a take. If you feel any resistance strike 'hard' immediately.

Some popular freshwater 'live' baits include: Roach, perch, rudd, dace, trout, tench, goldfish, stone loach, and bullhead's.

<u>MY SPECIAL SPRAT RIG...</u>

For dead-baiting I also favour using large, single circle hooks and 'longshank' seafishing hooks for sink and draw or 'wobbling' sprats. I hide the majority of the long (shank) of the hook inside the sprat (running right through the middle of it.) The eye of the hook comes out of the sprat's mouth. The point of the hook or "business end" rises out of the sprat's back just in front of or at the point of the dorsal fin. The hook point faces forward or towards the sprat's head.

<u>A SUPER SIMPLE SPRAT RIG...</u>

Another quicker, easier, way to do it is to simply stick a single size six treble hook straight in the back of the sprats head... It is not as safe or secure, but will get your bait straight back out into the water - double quick. This rig works best when a big pike suddenly appears in your swim out of nowhere and time is of the essence...

Sprats are easy to get hold of but they are soft bodied and will only last a few casts (6 - 12) unless they are used frozen. You can use them frozen and yes they are hard but then so are plastic, wood and metal lures and that never put anyone off using them. The trick is in timing the strike - if you feel anything, any resistance at all then do not hesitate - strike immediately and hard! Just like you would if using a lure - which in fact you are. You can easily incorporate your strike into your twitching/ retrieve. Trust me - this method is very effective and even wily old, shy pike that are very wary of modern lures/plugs will go for your bait without any hesitation whatsoever.

PREFERRED HOOK SIZE...

For pike and predator fishing: I favour using the larger treble hooks such as size 6's or even size 4's.

For smaller (mouthed) species of fish such as the trout I might use a smaller treble hook such as a size 8 or 10 . Chub and Perch have mouth's like buckets so hook size is generally not an issue but for the fish's welfare you might consider using a single hook on a bait such as a sprat or a smaller treble on a lure or dead-bait rig.

BARBLESS HOOKS...

I am not a big fan of 'barbless' hooks. Call me old fashioned but I prefer a good old fashioned barb or at the very least a 'micro' barb on my fishing hooks/trebles. It inspires me with more confidence.

Those trebles with only one barb on one hook are a bad invention/practically useless... What is more useful: Losing your fish or losing your bait on the cast? Answer: Neither!!

DEADBAIT HOOK RIGS

You can catch pike using two trebles or even three trebles on your deadbait rigs (It all depends on the size of your bait). Three trebles (or even singles/circle hooks) may sound like a lot of hooks but it all depends on what you are using for bait...

If you are using a single sprat then one hook may suffice. If you are using a full mackerel then three hooks may be necessary to ensure hooking on the strike. If you are using half a mackerel then two hooks may be sufficient.

DISTANCE IN BETWEEN HOOKS...

I would say that the optimum distance in between hooks on a live/deadbait rig is a minimum of at least four inches apart...

This is close enough to hook even a small, four or five pound jack pike.

Please bear in mind, that this is the minimum recommended distance. Please feel free to spread your hooks out further when in pursuit of 'big game.' But always bear in mind that you run the risk of losing a few jacks! (If your hooks are spread much further than four inches apart.)

WHAT TO DO WHEN THE FLOAT GOES UNDER...

There are two ways of approaching this... Traditional, 'conventional wisdom' says that you must 'wait' at least a few seconds for your pike float to go completely under the water and make off in the other (or any) direction. So as to give the pike time to turn and attempt to swallow the bait, thus maximising your chances of 'setting the hooks.' Before reeling in any and all available slack and then striking 'hard' (usually upwards) or 'diagonally' upwards in order to secure a good hook hold in the pike's hard, bony jaws. You then reel in any leftover slack created during the strike and keep the line tight and the rod bent into the fish, steadily applying 'pressure' to the fish and slowly, steadily, attempting to recover line and reel in the fish. Fishermen usually raise the rod to a vertical position, then drop the rod back down and quickly reel in some line then raise the rod again, then reel in some more line (ad infinitum) until the fish is played in/ tired out and lying on its side at the surface of the water ready to safely go in the net...

Or...

ALTERNATIVELY...

You could throw the rule book in the bin and do what I sometimes do (which is completely unorthodox.) I sometimes strike immediately - on first contact with the fish... (like you would do when lure fishing.) As soon as I know that the pike has my bait firmly secured in its mouth/jaws. Just don't completely jump the gun! Or you may lose a few fish this way (or you may not.) You may lose fish the other way...

I am just a bit of an odd ball and I like to use the lessons that I have learnt from lure fishing. Sometimes, unnecessary hesitation can be costly! Nobody ever waits for a pike to turn (and slowly swim away) with the lure held in its mouth! Listen, I am an a one off, I like to try new things, and do things a bit differently... You can successfully hook and catch fish either way!

LURE FISHING VS LIVE/DEADBAITING

These are the conclusions which I have drawn regarding the differences between lure fishing and live/dead baiting:

Lure fishing catches more fish but generally a smaller average size (usually less than ten pounds in weight.)

Live/dead baiting catches less fish but generally a bigger average size and the potential to catch ten pound plus, double figure and specimen fish (twenty pounds plus.)

Lure fishing requires more skill and sometimes a lot of skill.

Deadbaiting requires more patience and sometimes a lot of patience. Not to mention a good rig and good timing.

Sometimes, you have no choice but to live or dead bait to catch the really big pike. I know of two waters in particular where you can only regularly catch pike up to about 7 or 8 pounds on lures even though there are much bigger pike in these waters. You have two choices: catch lots of little ones on lures or catch a few big ones on live or deadbaits.

NATURAL BAITS

1. LOBWORM LURE RIG

You can easily turn a live lobworm into a big fat juicy lure... Just attach two hooks (one at each end.) Either ordinary coarse fishing hooks, two circle hooks, or two small treble hooks (size 8 - 10.) Then, just cast the worm out and reel it back in as if it was a lure. You can reel it in fast or slow but I prefer to fish it at depth and reel it in slowly or steadily... These rigs work excellently on small rivers/streams/canals or ponds and catch pike, perch, chub and trout as well as any fish that eats worms. The biggger the lobworm - the better! Don't forget to use a wire trace if there are any pike about...

2. WORMS - THE OCTOPUS RIG

Just pick the biggest, fattest, juiciest worms that you can get your hands on. Preferably lobworms but redworms (the stripey ones that wriggle like crazy when you handle/hook them) work well too. Place as many as you like onto a large single hook or a treble hook. You could use two or three lobworms for perch or chub or you could use six to a dozen worms for pike, carp and catfish. Attach a super bouyant float like a wine bottle cork or a 15 - 20 gram clear plastic/bubble float. set your depth at whatever depth you think the fish are primarily feeding at from one to four feet plus down. Bear in mind that many fish such as carp will feed on the surface and the bottom. Cast your bait into the horizon bearing in mind that the further away the bait is from you - the more confidant the fish will be taking it. set your baitrunner/drag, whether you sit back and relax or watch your float like a hawk - expect to catch something and more than likely - something big and out of the ordinary. A bigger bait generally attracts and catches a bigger fish.

3. FREELINED WORM ON THE BOTTOM.

This is a devastatingly effective method for catching wild river fish such as chub, perch, trout and other course fish like carp or barbel. Simply tie a decent sized hook (a size twelve or ten) onto your line with a good strong reliable knot such as a four or five turn grinner knot. Hook a worm in the middle. Make sure your hook has a decent barb on it or the worm may wriggle of the hook. You can hook the worm twice if this makes you feel more comfortable but remember that natural presentation is paramount. Another way to do it is to tie two hooks onto your line about five or six inches apart depending on the length of the worm. Cast the worm into the middle of the river or stream, leave your bale arm off so the river can take line freely and watch your line like a hawk. The moment line starts flying off your reel - you have a fish on. Strike immediately or wait a few seconds - the choice is yours. This method also works very well using floating bread (white.) Just watch your bread float down river/ stream and wait for something to rise up and take it. With bread it is best to strike fast as fish can steal the bread off your hook if you hesitate. This is a devastating method for wild trout and chub.

'MICROBAITING'

'Micro-baiting' simply means using small or 'micro' species of fish that anglers generally do not bother to fish for (or are uninterested in) as live or dead baits. Little fish such as the bullhead or millers thumb, stone loach, gudgeon, sticklebacks, minnows, and others make great baits floatfished alive or dead in small rivers/streams, canals, ponds or lakes.

Microbaits such as bullhead or miller's thumb, loach and gudgeon are bottom dwellers. They can all easily be caught in a large hand net...

You can expect to catch, chub, trout, perch, pike or indeed any other predator in the vicinity on these baits.

Try them they really do work wonderfully well... When using small/er live baits or 'micro' baits you can simply hook them in the bottom lip or in the tail. Rather than hooking small baits in the tail you can even use a tie wrap so you do not need the hook to penetrate the flesh of the bait. Just feed the tie wrap through the eye of the hook and wrap it around the tail root of the fish. 'Micro' baits (live or dead) can be hooked in the lip, back or tail. When striking - your strike should always be instantaneous. (You do not need to wait for the pike to rotate or 'turn' the bait the way you do when using a larger bait.)

FLOAT FISHED BULLHEADS

A bullhead or millers thumb is quite simply a small member of the catfish family that survives by living under rocks and feeding on tiny insects. They are well camouflaged and usually a black, brown, grey or muddy colour. They only grow to about four or at the most five inches long and are at the bottom of the foodchain. They can be found in large numbers in small streams and shallow rivers and lakes. They like fast flowing, well oxygenated water. They are often found living among loach, crayfish, trout and chub.

BULLHEAD PRESENTATION

Bullheads work best float-fished. As they are a naturally bottom dwelling fish and given half a chance will disappear underneath the nearest rock, bank, tree roots, or snag. A wine bottle 'cork' float is more than adequate or sufficient for float fishing live bullheads or other small fish. You could also use a bubble float (I favour the clear ones) or a pike float. You can tie wrap a single small treble hook (size 6, 8, or 10) to the root of the bullhead's tail to keep him lively in the water. Or put a small treble or single hook, (circle hook, long shank, or other) through the bullheads bottom lip. Bullhead's are fairly hardy little fish. I prefer to use as big a one as I can catch. A large one can last for hours fished in this way. The bullhead will attempt (unsuccessfully) to reach the bottom of the river, pond or lake periodically. Live float-fished bullheads will catch pike, perch, chub and trout as well as other freshwater predators. I have had great success on both float fished 'live' bullheads and ultra-realistic 'Salmo' bullhead lures. I have caught pike, perch and chub on 'Salmo' bullhead lures. All on the same outing. I have never tried bullhead deadbait but it is possible that they may work well fished in a sink and draw fashion.

TROUT AND CHUB ON THE BULLHEAD...

Bullheads make good live baits for trout and chub as they form a considerable portion of their natural diet alongside sticklebacks, minnows and other small fish fry or parr.

PERCH ON THE BULLHEAD...

Bullheads also make good live baits for perch of all sizes from 6 inches to specimen size. Simply plop one into one of the margins of the bank, or float fish one down stream or down river and if there is a perch there it will usually attack it on sight! Experience has shown that even a surprisingly small perch (6 inches in length) will attack and engulf a surprisingly large bullhead of 3 or 4 inches in length.

PIKE ON THE BULLHEAD...

Pike love bullheads! Nearly all fish are predators. The 1st law of nature is survival. Therefore all fish are by necessity opportunist feeders and the pike being at the very top of the foodchain has no qualms about feeding on his smaller brothers and sisters at the bottom of the foodchain. In nature, the bigger a pike, perch, chub or trout can grow by regular and opportunistic feeding - the less predator's he will have to watch out for and thus he has more chance of ensuring his survival. The same law also applies to a so called non predatory fish such as a carp or tench. The bigger he grows by regular and opportunistic feeding - the less predator's will see him as a potential meal.

CATCHING BULLHEAD'S FOR BAIT...

Bullheads are a bottom dwelling species of catfish commonly found in fast flowing, well oxygenated, rivers and streams. They can also be found on the bottom of ponds and lakes. They like the same sort of water conditions as trout, chub, crayfish, loach and other native species of coarse fish. They tend to live on gravel beds and underneath rocks and bricks on the river bed. They can also be found living in the silt/mud and underneath riverbanks. The easiest way to catch them for bait is with a large hand-net or landing net. Simply place the net behind a large rock or brick and then turn the rock/brick over and in the disturbance the bullhead's will swim downstream and straight into your net.

LOACH/STONE LOACH

You can also catch loach or 'stone' loach in the same way... Loach, sometimes called stone loach or weather loach by the pet shops are another small, bottom dwelling fish of similiar size to the bullhead. And also, of no real interest to anglers except maybe for bait...

Loach, also can grow to about four or five inches long. When disturbed, they are a much livelier, faster swimming fish than the bullhead. But, like the bullhead they prefer to live on the bottom amongst the gravel bed, and under stones and rocks. They can be used for bait but are a bit less common than the widely distributed bullhead. Both can be found living together in the same locations. The gudgeon is another small, bottom dwelling fish that makes great bait for pike, perch, chub and trout...

HOW TO MAKE HOME MADE FLOATS...

WINE BOTTLE 'CORK' FLOATS

Make a pike, carp, live or dead bait float from an old wine bottle cork and some paper clips or hair clips. Just fashion the paper clip into a one inch U shape and feed it carefully into a cork (using plyers.) I like to add a quick release clip for fast and convenient attachment of your float to your line. Carp are no more wary of cork floats than they are of any other piece of wood in their environment. In fact, I have had a double figure carp try to eat my cork float no less than three times! The other great thing about cork floats is that they cost nothing, they only weigh a few grams yet they are extremely buoyant and aerodynamic. You can cast them miles compared to an ordinary float. There are advantages to be had in using them especially when course fishing with light baits such as bread, sweetcorn, or worms. A cork float will even hold up large deadbaits like half a mackerel - no problem.

BALLOON FLOATS

This is a little known method which is a secret weapon of mine, it is both simple and ingenious...

You can also use an ordinary balloon as a float. Just blow it to size and then instead of just tying a granny knot. Tie the granny knot directly onto your line. This allows the 'float' to slide up and down your line easily to adjust fishing depth. You can use as big or as small a balloon as you like. The bigger the balloon the more the wind catches it thus allowing you to search out big lakes and gravel pits and cover lots of water. This enables you to search out and seek big pike or catfish proactively instead of just waiting for them to come to you. You can use a big, bright or black balloon for obvious sight indication or a smaller white, green or clear balloon for a more subtle, natural bait presentation. The great thing is that balloons cost next to nothing, they weigh next to nothing and they only take up a little room in your tackle box, with a balloon you can adjust your depth instantly and it is the simplest thing in the world to use. This is a trick that I should have probably just kept to myself...

THE FISH OF A LIFETIME!

One saturday morning, Me and my friend decided to go piking. He arrived at my home at 9.30am and we arrived at the waters edge at about 11 am. Both of us cast out float-fished deadbaits. My friend was using half a lamprey for bait and I was using a large, clear plastic, bubble float half filled with water (for extra casting weight) two size 4 treble hooks and two sprats. The sprats were hooked together by the tales on one treble (secured with a single tie wrap thread through the eye of the treble and wrapped tightly around both fish tails.) The other treble was hanging loosely between the fish nearer the heads.

We cast out into two different spots to the left and to the right of a central island opposite our peg. We left the floats and baits in position in the centre of some channels in between three islands. Hoping that if any big pike were on the move then sooner or later they would stumble upon our baits. It was a stifling, red hot day. My friend decided to doze off and take a little nap or two in his chair. I was bored and restless by about two o clock. By ten to five, nothing had happened all day and I really was fed up at this point! We had been fishing for about 6 hours with absolutely nothing to show for it. I was restless, bored, dehydrated, disheartened and completely demoralised. I turned and said to my friend. "If nothing has happened by five o clock then we should head home." "Agreed" he said. I should have known better, this water was notorious for fishing better or 'best' in the evenings...

AT A TIME THAT YOU THINK NOT...

I had given up on fishing by this point. I was busy talking and wishing away the time until five o clock came, completely convinced that we had blanked. All of a sudden, out of the corner of my eye, I saw my line absolutely flying off the reel! "What on earth!" I said. To give you some idea how freely my line was flying off the reel the only comparison I can make is when you take your bale arm off and cast out! That's about the size of what that pike was doing to my line.

If I had left my bale arm on my reel, then I have no doubt whatsoever that I would have never seen that rod and reel again! It would have gone waterskiing around the lake! I picked up my rod and looked out onto the lake to where my bubble float had been sitting all day. It was still visible above water, but it was flying off to the right, down a channel, towards the far island on the right. This presented a big problem for me as there was an overhanging tree in the water to the right of me and the fish had already flew past it "What shall I do?" I said to my friend. "strike" he said "you've got no choice!"

I didn't want to strike yet as I was convinced that this was a really big pike and she hadn't even taken my float underwater properly yet! With hindsight, I should have just struck hard right away but like I say I was caught completely off guard. Still, I had to do something, I had no choice because of the overhanging tree. If she tangled me up in it then I would lose the fish of a lifetime for sure. Without a second to think I raced into the water in front of me and walked out as far as I could to keep the fish from pulling my line into the overhanging tree. At last, I struck as hard as I could and began to reel furiously, trying to recover line and connect with this big fish. Guess what happened? The big pike didn't even bat an eyelid! She just carried on her run straight down the channel to my right. The only difference was - now, instead of line flying off my reel, my bale arm was on. I was standing knee deep in water (silty water I might add) soaked to the knees and reeling furiously to try and make contact with this beast of a fish! The only problem was, I couldn't seem to do it! The faster I reeled, the more my drag seemed to scream out in protest and the more line the fish took! I had set my drag to what I thought was an appropriate level before I started fishing. It was set to give line 'begrudgingly' but now it was giving line freely - almost willingly. I could not believe the power of this fish! I had no choice, I knew what I had to do...

I had to take a chance and tighten my drag in the middle of fighting this fish! I did it as quickly as I could and I'm sure it must have only taken me a second or two. I finally connected with the fish and it felt very strong! She thrashed left and right and then she was gone! I looked out to my right, towards the corner of an island and I could see all this clay that had been churned up off the bottom, then I saw this long, torpedo shaped shadow skulk off down the channel. I had lost her. I had lost what must certainly have been my personal best pike and quite possibly the fish of a lifetime... and I never really stood a chance because I was caught so off guard! I couldn't believe it. I was absolutely gutted. It's times like this when I feel like giving up fishing! It can be so demoralising! I waited for hours on end for my chance to come and then when it does come, I go and completely mess it up! Typical. There is one thing that I will say: I have never had a pike take like that in all my life and if the reel hadn't given line at that moment, when that fish took off on that incredible, unstoppable run then I am certain that my line probably would have broken anyway... Don't get me wrong. I was using good quality, strong, reliable 12 pound line that has never let me down before in the past but that fish and that run was something else...

She just seemed to take off on an unstoppable run. "Something's gotta give" as they say. I did carry on fishing for another couple of hours after that but nothing eventful happened.   I'll get you next time gadget, as the saying goes. I may have lost the battle but I'll win the war is another saying that springs to mind and next time I'll be better prepared. Forewarned is forearmed as they say.

To be honest, I do think my drag was set correctly - to give line very grudgingly, as is my usual custom but that fish was something else. It was an incredibly strong fish. I made a few schoolboy errors that day... The main errors I made were:

Running out of patience, losing confidence in my methods, followed by giving up in the middle of a session, and not fully concentrating on the job in hand. It was my lapse in concentration that really let me down and that ultimately led to me losing that fish. It may sound like I am making excuses but the truth of the matter is that I waited all day and then hooked and lost that big pike all in a matter of a minute... But hey that's fishing!

CHAPTER 12. NIGHT FISHING FOR PIKE AND CATFISH

<u>NIGHT FISHING...</u>

If you are planning on night fishing or fishing on for a couple of hours into darkness... Then make sure that you pack torches, head-lamps, electronic bite alarms and plenty of spare batteries. Also, make sure that you have a fully charged mobile phone with plenty of credit and that your loved ones know exactly where you are. It is best not to fish alone after dark. Especially in winter when the water can be freezing cold!

Take food and drink with you, stay hydrated and just as a precaution... Make sure that somebody knows exactly where you are at all times.

<u>THE 'WITCHING' HOUR</u>

A few years ago, I noticed something important in my fishing: You don't catch Jacks at night. The Jacks seem to switch off at nightfall and the big pike seem to come out and play. At night, the Jacks go and hide and the big pike come out to hunt. If you hook a pike at night, the chances are that it is going to be a big pike. It's like crocodiles and catfish - they are nocturnal, they come out at night. I'm not saying that you can't catch a big pike or a catfish in daylight hours, by all means you can! What I am saying is this: If you hook a fish on a lure, live or deadbait while night fishing under the cover of darkness. It isn't going to be small. It's more than likely going to be a big female pike, a catfish or a zander. The really big predators use the cover of nightfall to hunt more efficiently. The darkness helps them to sneak up closer on their prey. Some of them hunt by moonlight... This is because: At night/under the cover of darkness... Small fish lose the confidence to hunt and are more inactive/passive. Just laying low and taking cover. Whilst (or because) the big predators are at their most dangerous... Almost imperceptible, supremely confident and highly active...

NATURES CLOCK...

How do you know when the Jacks are looking for a place to hide and the monsters are coming out of their lairs? I will tell you. Nature has her own clock and it is very precise and reliable... When the lobworms are surfacing from their holes. When the bats start homing in on your surface poppers! When the foxes come out of their holes... and when the big toads start a croaking... Thats when the big boys (and girls!) come out to play...

THE 'WELS' CATFISH AS 'SUPREME' HUNTER...

The wels catfish is at the very top of the food chain... A super efficient, highly successful, ultra 'dominant' top end predator... That will see "almost anything" as a potential food source! Live or dead. Fresh or not so fresh... Fish, birds, mammals - you name it! It's all on the menu...

Do not be deceived by the catfish's sluggish shape, apparant 'slow' movements, or strange appearance... They are 'devastating' ambush predators. Known to even predate successfully upon large birds such as pigeons and ducks! At close range and over a short distance, they are highly powerful, 'explosive' hunters. Make no mistake about it. Contrary to what some people might think... When pike and catfish occupy the same territory... The pike is no longer the 'apex' predator (at the very top of the food chain) - the catfish is!! (the top end predator!) The catfish has the ability to make the pike's life and survival very difficult for him! As well as competing for the same food sources - fish, birds, mammals, amphibians or rodents, (both live and dead.) The catfish has a superior sense of smell and will actively swim and hunt during night time hours - under the cover of complete darkness. (The pike hunts more during daylight hours.) As well as this, the catfish will also actively hunt, ambush and predate upon the pike himself! It is true that the pike will also hunt and predate upon young, smaller, juvenile catfish. But most importantly in the animal kingdom/fish world - the catfish has a bigger mouth! And so ultimately, the catfish has a greater overall maximum size, weight and growth potential! One thing I will say though: The catfish wouldn't stand a chance in a beauty contest! The catfish may be 'ugly' but (like the pike) they are still an awesome predator to behold...

TAILS AND FINS

The pike may have an impressive 'muscular' tail and large, 'fast propulsion' tail fins for hunting (and evading danger) but the catfish is simply something else... The catfish's tail (and tail fin) is much longer and contains much more musculature than the pike's or any other fish for that matter. This is why catfish are such great fighters and make such excellent sporting fish! Their tails and tail fins go on for feet, not just inches!

TINY EYES (NOT PRIMARILY A 'SIGHT' FEEDER.)

Catfish are 'primarily' but not exclusively nocturnal (night time) hunters. However, catfish are very different from other predators such as the pike, perch, zander etc. Pike are primarily 'sight feeders.' They have large eyes, excellent eyesight and binocular vision (which simply means - they can see best in front and above them.) Perch too have large eyes and excellent vision. Zander too have large eyes but they are more well suited to night time hunting than most other predators such as the pike or the perch. Unlike other predators, the catfish does not have large eyes, and is not predominantly a 'sight' feeder... The catfish actually has small, 'beady' little, (tiny) eyes. (When you compare the size of the catfish's head and body with its eyes.)

'UNIQUE' LONG WHISKERS

So, with that being said: How does the catfish make up for this? How does it hunt and feed so efficiently? And how are they able to grow to such a large size? well first of all a catfish has something that a pike, perch, zander, chub and trout do not have... Can you guess what it is? It's pretty obvious really... Whiskers!! Big, long, extended whiskers. Sometimes, well over a foot long... Hence where they get the name catfish. A catfish is a little bit like a snail or a slug. If you have ever seen a snail/slugs whiskers. These scavengers (natures clean up crew) are excellent at homing in on unwanted food items. The catfish uses these long impressive whiskers to feel things in the dark and to help it to locate (and hunt) its food.

A HIGHLY DEVELOPED SENSE OF SMELL

The other thing a catfish has (more than other predatory fish) is a super sense... A 'super' highly developed sense of smell. A bit like a great white sharks ability to 'smell blood' over long distances... The catfish can easily 'home in' on potential food sources and items over very long distances...

CATFISH BAITS, GROUNDBAITS AND SCENTS...

The catfish can easily smell any dead, diseased or rotting fish or meat from a relatively long distance away. Such as the opposite side of a large lake or pond or a long way down river from the potential food source! Hence the very high success rates of nocturnal anglers using smelly baits such as sea fish (mackerel, sprat, herring, sardine, smelt etc) squid, large, high leakage (super smelly) fish pellets, such as halibut (a large sea fish) pellets and other fish pellets, smelly baits, fish attractors and various 'scents' which are readily available online and in most fishing tackle shops and come in a weird, 'wacky' and wonderfully wild range of highly concentrated, powerful, and 'potent' scents.

The catfish is not a fussy eater and a bit like a crocodile or alligator will even gravitate towards and happily eat - meat (such as chicken) that is past its best, on the turn, going off, gone off, or even dare I say it 'rancid.' That may be the case with the catfish but I would NEVER recommend handling or using baits such as this due to the obvious high risks (germs, bacteria, food poisoning, infection etc.) By all means use smelly (fresh) baits, sea fish/baits, squid etc... Just make sure your baits are clean and fresh! You have to put your own health and welfare first! If the catfish is a living garbage/waste disposal unit... Willing (and able) to eat "just about anything" - and still survive/thrive - that is its problem! It doesn't mean you should take any unnecessary chances! By all means: Be inventive, be creative, use your imagination, be resourceful. try all manner of baits and 'groundbaits.' Just stay safe! Try (regular) shrimps or prawns, king prawns... A great load of chopped worms might make an attractive 'smelly' groundbait. As might blended/liquidised or chopped up sprats or mackerel. A load of large worms on a large hook will also make a very attractive bait! Both due to the 'nasty' smell and the constant wriggling!! The large worm offering should soon be "homed in on" and picked up by the catfish's excellent sense of smell and/or long sensitive whiskers... Just remember, as a general rule: Bigger baits attract bigger fish!! So slap 'plenty' of worms on the hook... The more the better!!

HOOK SIZE

At the risk of stating the obvious... Catfish have very large (rough textured) mouths. So, you need to upscale your hooks. Not just because of the size of the fish's mouth but because catfish are such big, strong, powerful fish and great fighters. You must use strong hooks. Either regular, standard 'longshank' sea fishing type hooks, large treble hooks, or large circle hooks. One hook may not be enough. You may need two!!

LINE STRENGTH AND POTENTIAL SNAGS...

Again, you may need to 'upscale' the thickness and strength of the fishing line you are using quite considerably... Depending on the size (length and weight) of the fish you are targeting and the amount of potential snags in the immediate vicinity. Not just because catfish are big, long, heavy and strong (and great fighters) but because catfish are a territorial fish that live in dens or 'hidey' holes under the banks and amongst many thick, strong, winding tree roots. Once hooked, catfish are notorious for heading straight for their refuge or other large 'snags.' They are powerful enough as it is, due to the length and thick musculature of their tails and tail fins. Throw in a fallen log, some winding tree roots, and a few other snags and you could be in serious trouble landing one!

BACKWARDS IN COMING FORWARDS...

Another unique feature of the catfish is their ability to swim backwards!! You have to be ready and expect this! A catfish (unlike many other fish) will not just get tired, go easy, or just lie on the surface of the water belly up waiting for you to net it! No sir. When you reel them in towards the bank and they finally catch sight of you... Standing over them, large net in hand, they will immediately begin swimming backwards, away from the bank, away from you, and away from your net! If you have never fished for catfish before... You have to be prepared for this. A large one will not come in easy, submit or surrender when he or she is close to the bank. Nope. It is on!! So expect a bit more of a struggle and a potentially longer fight. With this being said: Catfish can be a bit trickier to land or 'bank' so having a fishing accomplice on hand can be very useful!

BEAUTY AND THE BEAST...

One evening, me and an old friend decided to do a little night fishing. We loaded up my friends car with everything but the kitchen sink and set off in search of some big pike and catfish...

We drove out into the countryside, past a couple of picturesque little villages, and arrived at the lakes just as the sun was setting. It was a beautiful night - a perfect night, one of those nights that makes you feel glad just to be alive. The lakes were eerie and atmospheric. You could feel the electricity in the air.

We had just about enough time to set up before the sun went down. We decided to target two lakes that were back to back... I set up my rod and reel and cast out as far I could towards the centre of the lake on my right. My bait hit the surface of the water with a loud splash. It's ripples crashing through the dream like calm of the lake's peace and serenity. I had on half a herring (the tail end) with two size four trebles, a foot long wire trace (for the pike) and a 'cork' float set at about four foot deep. I set my bite alarms and settled in for a long night...

As the hours rolled by I sat back in my chair and began to daydream... I thought back to one sunny summers day, several years ago when I was sneaking around this exact same lake attempting to stalk fish. I was creeping through some small trees on a strip of island that ran between two lakes. I sneaked through carefully with my army camouflage gear on and my green wellington boots. As I reached the centre of the right hand lake, I stood at the waters edge looking out over the lake surveying the scene, and looking for any signs of life. The sun was very bright and the water was crystal clear. I stood perfectly still and breathed it all in, I was in my element, at one with nature - I felt alive.

Out of the corner of my eye I sensed movement. I looked down, and right below me, just coming into my field of vision was a strange, dark brown, mottled, slug like shape, wobbling along slowly around the perimeter of the lake. It was a catfish. My estimate is in the region of three to four feet in length. I only had a precious few moments to observe this strange creature that was literally at my feet! It swam or should I say 'wobbled' along slowly with a lure like motion and didn't seem to be in an a rush or have a care in the world.

This was the first time that I had seen a catfish swimming in the water in this way. I honestly believe that the catfish most probably did not know that I was there, or at least not until the last second. The catfish swam along the edge of the bank leisurely and then turned off the pinnacle where I was standing and headed out across the lake. Wow I thought to myself, you don't see that everyday! The last thing I remember seeing is that great, long tail rippling along in the water. I'd never 'stalked' a catfish before, It definitely gave me something to think about...

That was about five years ago, and it was with that memory fresh in my mind that I had cast out my half a herring. "Hopefully, we'll meet again" I thought to myself.

The sound of my bite alarm beeping brought me back to reality in a flash. "Now that's what I'm talking about" I thought to myself. I jumped up out of my camping chair and ran in the direction of the beeping sound and the little red light. I lifted my rod and 'felt' my line running through my fingers at a pace. "Oh yes" I thought to myself, "this is some run." I struck 'hard' lifting my rod tip right up into the air. "Fish on" I shouted. My rod was bent double into this fish but it was just defying me and taking off on an unstoppable run. I felt the weight of it - It felt like a very heavy fish. "This is a big fish" I said to my buddy "a very big fish," feeling it's power. My friend panicked, he was rifling through all my pockets, desperately trying to lay his hands on a torch! Whilst I did my best to ignore this intrusion and concentrate on the job in hand...

Out in the middle of the lake the fish broke the surface, splashing on the top of the water. Neither of us could see any thing at this point as it was pitch black but I could FEEL that this fish was huge. The fish was trying to steam off towards an island on my far left, whilst I pulled to my right and piled on the pressure. I hoped my hooks and line would hold. I was only using nine pound line (sylcast) top quality stuff though... Meanwhile my friend was running up and down the bank desperately trying to lay his hands on my fishing net! As I turned this huge beast around my buddy appeared next to me holding the net. It was finally coming in and we were both about to see it up close for the first time... I secretly hoped that it was a huge pike as it would have been my personal best... It wasn't. It was a catfish - a huge beast of a catfish! "What an ugly mother......" I said. "That's exactly what I thought" my friend said. My friend then attempted to net the catfish which would have measured about five feet long... "What are you doing?" I said. "You can't net that - it'll snap the net!" "What are you going to do then?" he said. "I'll chin it" I said. I stepped down the steep bank, placed my left welly in the water and chinned the big cat with one hand. My friend then proceeded to bear hug me and attempted to lift both me and the catfish back up onto the bank. "What are you doing?" I said. "Helping you back up" he replied! "I don't need any help!" I said. I lay the big cat down gently and unhooked it with my (multitool) plyers.

Luckily for me, both hooks were in solid so I hadn't lost my hookhold during the battle. "What a big mouth" I thought to myself and "what big rubbery lips!" I noticed that the fish had tiny, 'beady' little eyes and huge whiskers - two of which were easily over a foot long. I said to my buddy "you return this fish to the water for me as I want you to feel the weight of it..." He returned the fish for me. "Well, what do you reckon?" I asked, "About forty pounds" he replied. "exactly" I said. I looked at the time. It was about twelve thirty am. It had taken a good three or four hours to get that run. Apart from that it was an uneventful night. It was freezing cold, we had no more runs and we caught no more fish. We lay shivering in the tent until first light (seven am) while it rained all night. Then we drove home to catch up on our sleep!

Sometimes I wonder to myself... Could it be the exact same fish that I saw that sunny, summers day - five long years ago?

A few years later... I showed some photographs of the catfish to another friend of mine. Who is a more experienced 'cat' fisherman than me... "What do you reckon then?" I said. "It's a good fish, he said, judging from the photos, it's at least forty pounds, could be forty five." In england (where I live) the wels catfish is not a native species and are not as widespread and readily available to catch as they are in America and Europe (where they can grow much bigger, sometimes weighing hundreds of pounds.) Where I live, in England, a 40 - 45 pound catfish whilst being pretty modest for the rest of the world is in fact pretty big for us brits!

CATCHING BIG CATFISH ON SOFT BODIED SHADS OR "JELLY" LURES

There is really nothing to it. Just select a rubber fish lure sometimes known as a shad or a jelly lure. Remove the bottom treble - if there is one, to stop you getting your lure snagged on the bottom. Find a deep, dark 'catfishy' looking spot. Cast your lure out as close to the bank as you can without getting snagged. Let the lure sink for several seconds till it reaches as near to the bottom as you can safely get it without getting snagged. A good rule is to count one second per foot of water, so if the water is six feet deep then cast out your lure and when it has hit the water, count to six before retrieving it as s-l-o-w-l-y as possible.

The aim is to keep the lure down deep near the bottom where the catfish are most likely to be laying up. Most takes come on the drop or near/underneath the bank. Remember, strike hard! Another method is to cast out along the near bank either to your right or your left, and reel your lure along the edge of the bank as slowly as possible, and as close to the bank or even underneath it as you can get it. You can work your way around a whole pond or lake in this manner as catfish also like to actively 'patrol' the borders of their territory, hunting and scavenging for food. Catfish can be found in similiar locations to pike and you are just as likely to hit a pike as a catfish with these methods - if the pike are there.

<u>THE LAIR OF THE CATFISH</u>

Remember, by day the catfish are likely to be laid up in deep water, in the shadows, out of the sunlight, beneath undercut banks or overhanging trees or in amongst winding, twisted tree roots, fallen trees or logs, and other snags that afford them shade and cover. It is highly unlikely that you will be able to get your lure 'inside' their actual lair so you just have to be content to get it as close as possible to the entrance or at least somewhere in the proximity of the resting, inactive catfish. Catfish will actively guard the entrance to their lairs and any potential intruders will be met with a very hostile, aggressive response. If the water is muddy, brown or heavily discoloured due to recent heavy rains, or it is winter or a grey, cloudy, overcast day or approaching sunset then the catfish may not even be laid up inside their lairs. They may already be out and about actively hunting or feeding. Remember that catfish unlike pike are NOT primarily sight feeders so it does not really matter so much about water discolouration. This will not affect their ability to intercept your lures as catfish heavily rely on sound/vibration to locate prey as well as their incredible sense of smell.

<u>NIGHT FISHING FOR PIKE AND CATFISH</u>

Catfish are mainly nocturnal predators. They favour deep, dark water. They like to lie in the shadows... They have small eyes and poor eyesight but they more than make up for this with a highly developed sense of smell and sound (vibration.) They are hunter/scavengers. They have large sand paper like mouths with abrasive pads inside them. Their mouths are very hard and leathery with big, bony, rubbery lips... They have long whiskers (hence the name catfish) which help them to locate food/prey. They are elongated, powerful fighters and very efficient predators feeding on fish, amphibians and small birds and mammals. Their diet is very similiar to the pike's and they both thrive in a very similiar environment, thus you can easily fish for both species at the same time if and when they are both present in the same water. Catfish have a very inique swimming feature... They are able to swim or 'fight' swimming backwards which makes them harder to net, land or bank successfully. You get them near the bank but the battle is not yet over... They avoid the net by swimming backwards!

<u>A WAITING GAME</u>

You do everything exactly the same as you would when deadbaiting during daylight hours... The only difference is - you can barely see!! And neither can the fish. The fish rely on their sense of smell or vibration. Catfish have a very powerful sense of smell, and pike have a similiar but maybe not quite as sophisticated sense of smell. Pike rely on their 'neuromast' system to actively hunt (a kind of sensory radar built into their skull/face.) Not unlike an owl... And their lateral line (a sensory line which runs down both sides of the fish for sensing movement or vibration in the water.) You have to bear in mind that fish do not have ears... So think of the lateral line as the equivalent of our hearing. Does it work? You betcha! I have caught a large pike on a six inch lure in complete darkness - so yeah, it works!

The darkness presents a bit of a problem when attempting intricate little details like tying hooks or wire traces to your mainline... You have got to get yourself organised and set up during daylight hours before the sun goes down... After that, It's a waiting game... You may get a run in half an hour, or more likely... Several hours later, or even just before or even at sunrise! Patience is the name of the game.

THE NEUROMAST SYSTEM

When I was a young kid fishing Newstead Abbey for pike. We once caught a pike and upon close inspection we noticed that he had lots of deep, little holes or indentations on his face and around his eyes, mouth and under his chin. We naturally thought that this pike had been grabbed headfirst by another, bigger pike! We were wrong. These holes are part of the neuromast system and help the pike to hunt in the darkness. These holes are basically sensors which help the pike to intercept prey. After all to catch prey in his mouth, his movements have got to be very accurate and very precise. He has to be very alert and responsive to movement. He has to have 'lightning fast reflexes' to catch his prey and to avoid capture. I have caught pike on more than one occasion that are blind in one eye. Some of them big, old pike... By all accounts a pike can still hunt using the neuromast system, his lateral line and sound and vibration even if he is completely blind. I once caught a big pike on a lure at night and in complete darkness...

LAMPING

One night, whilst deadbaiting on my favourite lake, on my favourite peg, where I lost the big one, an old friend passed by. "I hope you can swim" he said. "What do you mean?" I asked. "There's fish in there that'll pull you in and take you waterskiing" he said. "Don't I know it" I thought to myself. "How do you know?" I asked. "I comedown here at night lamping." he said. "What's lamping?" I asked. "I come down here at night with a high powered lamp" he said "and you would be amazed at what I have seen." "Do you catch them?" I asked "No, I just watch them" he said. Now, why didn't I think of that? I thought to myself. Duh. That'll take the guess work out of night fishing!

ESSENTIAL ITEMS FOR NIGHT FISHING

Obviously you will need all your regular kit but with a dozen or so extra 'essential' items...

Hand torches (and batteries.) Bite alarms (and batteries.) Bank sticks, rod rests, head lamps (and batteries.) Tents, glow in the dark 'float' sticks, warm coats and clothing, water proof clothing/trousers, sleeping bags, foam 'roll' mats, drinks, food, snacks, smelly baits such as halibut pellets, sea fish (mackerel, sprats etc.) Squid, a large tub or bucket of large lob worms (night crawlers) or whatever scented 'groundbait' you can concoct during daylight hours... A large 'mouthed' long-handled landing net, wellington boots or thigh waders, a life jacket or highly buoyant vest/bodywarmer, strong rods, strong line, large (strong) hooks, long wire traces or leaders...

Always remember the 6 ps... Prior preparation prevents piss poor performance!!!

Joking aside. Keep it simple and don't overcomplicate things: You just need a big smelly (stinky) 'obvious' bait (presentation is no longer as important.) Then put it in the most likely, 'fishy' location. Then, you just need the patience of Saint Francis... Stay alert, stay ready! Don't fall asleep, or let your guard down!

CHAPTER 13.
OBSERVING PIKE, PERCH, CHUB & STICKLEBACK'S IN TANKS

Let me start by saying that there is no 'pseudo-science' here. Everything is based on my own personal research, first hand experience and many, many hours of keen observation... To put it simply...

I had to get my own hands dirty...

<u>PIKE FEEDING HABITS...</u>

Having kept pike, perch, chub and most other native course species in tanks (for about 14 years) for educational and observational purposes...

I can tell you that the smaller a fish is the more fully absorbed/engrossed it is by what is going on in it's immediate environment and the less it cares about what is going on outside of the aquarium environment, i.e my prying eyes! Small fish are seemingly oblivious to your presence, even if you are so close to them that your nose is almost pressed up against the glass!

The larger a fish is the more aware/self conscious it becomes...

A one inch pike is oblivious to it's observer... A ten inch pike knows that you are there, and a six inch pike is somewhere in between the two... Not completely oblivious, but not overly concerned. The bigger fish get - the more 'conscious' and wary, even when raised in captivity.

TINY 'MICRO' PIKE AND FREEZE DRIED BLOODWORMS

When I first started keeping little tiny, 'micro' pike the most obvious, logical thing to feed them on was worms or to be more specific - brandlings.

Later on, as I became more experienced (at catching them) and caught smaller and smaller pike. I needed something even smaller to feed them... I knew that if I could get some 'live' blood worms from the local pet shop then these would be a winner. There were none available so I tried what was available... Freeze dried bloodworms!

Imagine my surprise when these little tiny pike began scooping up and eating dead bloodworms! New born pike and already they were eating deadbait! These tiny newborn pike were in a tank with lots of sticklebacks which were actually bigger than the pike! The pike did not eat the bloodworms straight away but after a while I noticed that they were in fact eating them. It is quite possible that the pike learnt from observing the sticklebacks who took to eating the bloodworms like a duck to water...

'MICRO' PIKE VERSUS 'MICRO' PIKE

Over the years, I have kept numerous 'micro' pike of a similiar size in the same aquarium environment...

I have had three or four in the same tank at the same time... Contrary to popular belief, I have never seen one micro pike stalk or attempt to predate upon another. Never. The majority of the time they simply co-exist, ignore each other, avoid each other, or simply 'tolerate' each other. They would not stalk or attack each other (unless there was a considerable size differentiation.) There never is as I am very careful about this.

The young pike are however 'wary' of each other and reluctant to swim directly towards each other or 'face off.' If the young pike do swim past each other (they prefer not to) and feel threatened by one another, then they will enlarge their heads so as to appear larger than they really are so as to dissuade the other pike from eating them. It is a strange phenomenon and really quite funny to watch! I never had the pike in a tank completely alone. I always had lots of other small fish swimming around (to mimic the pike's natural environment) so there was always plenty going on to distract the small pike from each other.

As I have already said earlier in this book... When I observed super tiny pike hunting in the wild... They were fixated on the tiny silver fish - not each other.

If you put two 12 inch pike in a large tank at the same time the outcome is the same... They do not try to eat each other, they simply learn to tolerate each other. Pike seem to have a high 'stress' tolerance in regards to being around other predatory fish of a similiar size.

PERCH, CHUB AND PIKE

Perch (and chub) however, seem to realize that the key to their survival lies in eating more readily available food sources than the pike and thus ensuring that they are always (slightly) too big to be eaten! It is a race for survival. Thus in the presence of a similiar sized pike they become opportunistic, greedy and gluttonous in order to survive. The pike's presence does seem to represent a source of 'stress' to the other (predatory) fish once he is big enough to become a threat to them. Chub and perch seem to realise (and recognise) that the pike is a much more efficient predator. A faster, more mobile and very accurate hunter. I think the same thing plays out in the wild. Thus perch and chub will learn to eat almost anything, to grow as fast as possible, in order to ensure their survival.

PIKE, LOBWORMS AND BRANDLINGS...

I have witnessed one small pike of about 12 inches in length and slightly less than a pound in weight eat about 20 small worms one after another...

He wasn't starving or particularly hungry at this time. He was simply taking advantage of an easy meal that did not require chasing or catching. I readily observed that he did not attack the smaller worms, he simply scooped them up in his mouth and swallowed them first time. The bigger lobworms of 12 inches or more in length he seized as if the 'prey' were capable of escaping. He had a particular way of eating them headfirst - like a fish, and if he was not quite happy with the way that he had caught the worm then he would spit them out and grab them again, two or three times, until he held them just right.

I also observed that after taking or eating a big lobworm, both pike and perch seem to 'eject' a type of brown, cloudy, dust from their gills, which I assume must be the soil from the inside of the worm.

PIKE AND TADPOLES

One time I caught some tadpoles in a local river and took them home as an easy meal for my small pike... He chased, caught, and swallowed them (one by one) without the least bit of difficulty... My pike took his time and picked them off one by one... He seemed to be in no apparant rush to eat them all in one sitting!

I think that tadpoles due to their small size, inherent vulnerability and 'tail wobbling' swimming patterns (not dissimilar to a lure) must make up quite a considerable part of a coarse fish's diet...

It seems obvious to me that the majority of tadpoles born/found in river, canal, pond or lake are essentially 'cannon fodder' for all manner of fish, including (but not limited to) pike, perch, chub and trout. Which is why the frogs lay so many eggs... Not unlike fish!

REACTIVE HUNTING BEHAVIOUR

During the time that I was observing pike and perch in tanks, I noticed something really interesting. I kept a small pike and a large perch of about the same length in one aquarium. The perch is a much shyer fish than the pike and took about three days to come on the feed. The pike came on the feed within 15 - 20 minutes of being placed in the tank with live fish!

I also observed that "the perch turned the pike onto feeding" or the perch's predatory behaviour aroused and excited the pike's predatory instinct. If the perch chased or attacked a small fish, rather than hanging around in the background, the pike would be in the foreground and usually finish off any fleeing prey! I imagine it is much the same in the wild...

'YAWNING' OR JAW FLEXING...

Both the pike and the perch would sometimes appear to 'yawn' stretch, flex, or exercise their jaw muscles. This seemed to be the fish warming up and exercising their jaws in preparation to 'come on the feed.'

It seemed to be a reflex action for the perch every time he was around small, prey sized fish. I have also observed this strange phenomenon in the wild when a perch is preparing to 'strike' at prey fish. The perch never did this around lobworms, so my thinking is that he did it in preparation to attack and catch prey. It was as if he was suppressing or holding back his predatory urges to attack and feed because I was watching him.

The perch exhibited a Jekyll and Hyde personality. When he was not on the feed, he ignored everything going on around him and couldn't seem to care less about food or feeding. When he was hungry he became an altogether different animal and seemed to become a 'bully' and go on the rampage, prowling around, stalking fish and trying to drive them out of their hiding places and attacking anything in his path. This behaviour was always exhibited at night or as darkness fell. He mainly seemed to get hungry and want to feed at dawn or first thing in the morning and at dusk/sunset.

PIKE BEHAVIOUR (THE 'SHIMMY')

The pike is definitely a superior predator and a more efficient hunter than the perch owing to his more aerodynamic build and superior speed and accuracy.

The pike is not however *infallible, he does not always catch his prey.*

I have observed pike do what I call a 'shimmy' or sort of 'flex' when they are about to come on the feed. It is hard to describe this behaviour but they seem to go from a straight bodied position to a sort of muscular flex or 'ripple' that runs down the length of their entire body from the head to the tail. It only takes a few seconds to perform...

They do this as they are beginning to get hungry... It is a way of warming up their muscles for an attack or strike. I have never seen a pike do this in the wild but seen it many times whilst observing pike behaviour in an aquarium environment. The pike will even do it when there is no visible, available food or 'prey' source around. they like to stay 'ready' at all times...

Having kept pike for many years I know that this is a small 'tell' or indicator that the pike has when he is getting hungry or ready to feed.

Sometimes, the pike misses his prey and they get away. Sometimes he catches them and they manage to get away when he tries to turn them around to swallow them head first as is the pike's custom. The prey fish lay still and wait for their opportunity. When the pike momentarily releases his grip to get a better grip or turn the fish, the prey fish senses that this may be his last and only opportunity to escape and seizes the opportunity by swimming out of the pike's mouth and away from the pike at top speed. The pike rarely catches them, when they swim out of his mouth. He seems to sense that his opportunity has gone. Sometimes the prey fish having experienced an encounter like this will survive, although stressed, traumatized, bruised and wounded.

Other times, it is too much and the prey fish will swim away and escape only to die later of its injuries. Thus is the balance of nature. That is why you often see in the wild: Roach, chub and pike with cuts, wounds and scars from previous encounters with pike which they have miraculously survived. This is also why pike like to single out prey that are sick, ill, diseased, or dying. They are simply cashing in on previous encounters. Reaping the rewards of another pike's hard work, or following up old leads if you will.

One thing I will say is this: All fish (even roach and stickleback's) can be surprisingly resilient - even after suffering an unpleasant encounter with a hungry pike!

Some fish are more resilient and hardy than they look - such as roach. Each species is different. Some are surprisingly resilient and hardy, others are much more delicate.

THE FIRST LAW OF NATURE IS SURVIVAL AT ALL COSTS.

THE SECOND IS ECONOMY OF EFFORT OR MAXIMUM REWARD FOR MINIMUM EFFORT.

That is why a river trout, chub or pike faces upstream and waits for the river to bring him his food. Facing upstream also makes it easier for them to breathe. Pike and perch are ambush predators. They much prefer to lie in wait for unsuspecting prey than to chase them all over the place!

PIKE ARE 'COLD-BLOODED' (LITERALLY)

However, fish are cold blooded, therefore they become more active as the temperature increases and less active as the temperature cools. Thus their feeding/dietary requirements increase or decrease with the seasons and the temperature. Pike (like many other freshwater or 'course' fish) can sometimes be found 'basking' in the sun in shallow water or at the top of the water column in the warmer summer months. Another reason for this is because the warmer the water gets the less oxygen there is in the water! So the pike may be at the top of the water (the top foot) to bask in the sun and raise their body temperature before aggressively coming on the feed. Or (in the case of still waters/ponds) they may just need/crave more oxygen due to the increased heat!

I have also noticed that pike and other predatory fish such as the perch, trout and chub have accelerated (faster) growth rates once they begin eating other fish regularly or 'exclusively.'

PERCH BEHAVIOUR

I once read in one of the 'all knowing' popular fishing magazines... That a perch's stripes disappear when they die. This is not strictly true. Having kept two perch in the same tank at the same time I can tell you that one perch may display dark black stripes and the other may display no stripes at all whatsoever - none (Whilst it is still alive and well.) It has nothing to do with whether it is alive or dead but rather all depends on the perch's mood. In fact a perch's stripes can disappear, reappear, go darker and darker until black and back again and everything in between and none of this has anything to do with the perch being dead! It all depends on the fish's mood!

THE PERCH AS 'HUNTER'

The perch, though slower and less mobile than the pike, is an equally aggressive fish. The smaller perch like to chase their prey actively and have several snaps at their tails to 'stun' or disable them before eating them. Even large (3 or 4 pounds plus) trout can at times display exactly the same behaviour.

You can sometimes feel this pecking or snapping at your spinner or lure when a small perch is in pursuit of it. Trout do the same thing. I have observed two - three pounds plus trout attacking plugs and spinners in much the same way - quick, rapid fire attacks or 'nips' at the lure one after another in quick succession. I once saw a large trout (2 feet/24 inches plus long and 3 - 4 pounds in weight) attack my spinner from side to side, left, right, left, right, left, right, and so on, over and over again... (He was trying to 'incapacitate' or disable his prey.)

PREY 'INHALATION'

The bigger perch is a totally different story. A big perch approaches slowly and likes to 'corner' his prey. They are awesome to watch, and seem to bully or intimidate smaller fish with their mere presence. They creep up slowly and deliberately. Then, when they are about an inch or so away from their prey, they suck them in and engulf them whole with an awesome finality. (They inhale them or hoover them up with their mouths.) The sound is audible in an aquarium, it is like the sound a smooth stone or pebble makes when it is thrown into the water with great force - a thump or 'whooshing' sound. This is created by the 'vacuum' or the sudden 'whoosh' of water, into the perch's mouth and simultaneously out of his gills.

I have caught large 'specimen' perch on spinners, sometimes the bigger 12 - 15g spinners with quite big blades. Sometimes, when this has happened, the fish has sucked the spinner in deep to the back of the throat. He has tried to 'swallow it whole' as it were. When this has happened, often times I have had to unclip the quick release on my wire leader, and feed the spinner, hook, blade, wire leader and all out of the side of the perch's gill. This was the easiest and most logical way to unhook the perch.

The good thing about the big perch's style of taking his prey is that they very rarely come off the hook, when using spinners and plugs, and you rarely need to strike. They simply 'engulf' your lure with their big bucket mouths! I have seen small three to four inch perch, large bullhead's, and even four to five inch sprats instantly disappear in a perch's mouth. Even a relatively small six inch perch will quickly engulf a three - four inch perch on sight!

PERCH AND LOBWORMS...

It was during this time that I had a realization: People think that lobworms are a great bait for perch and they are right. I kept a 'specimen' perch that could eat 7 or 8 of the biggest Lobworms that you could find back to back within two seconds of each other when he was on the feed. He sucked them up like spaghetti. Sometimes he would grab the head or the tail of the worm and didn't seem to care which. Sometimes he would grab them in the middle and suck them in. *I never managed to get him to eat a dead worm.* (So much for artificial or rubber worms.) He wasn't interested in anything that didn't move or wasn't alive.

LIVEBAITS ARE THE BEST BAITS FOR 'SPECIMEN' PERCH

Do you know what he loved and preferred to eat more than anything else? What excited him the most? Live fish! He could resist the urge to attack or eat a worm. He could never resist a live fish though. Worms - he could take them or leave them. Fish - he would just take them and seemed utterly compelled to do so. Whether this was a territorial thing or a predatory thing I could not tell for sure. Possibly a combination of both.

I have witnessed both perch and pike kill fish and then leave them dead on the bottom so I am convinced that fish can behave very aggressively due to overwhelming territorial instincts or sometimes attack out of aggression or agitation rather than genuine hunger.

After having observed perch in an aquarium environment, I do believe, that you would stand a much better chance of catching the british record perch (or your own personal best perch) on a live fish than on a lobworm.

It is life itself and especially movement that seems to arouse the predatory instinct in pike, perch and other predatory fish. It is ironic that the very thing that a livebait does (i.e. get distressed or panic) is the self same thing that excites and arouses the predatory instinct in both pike, perch and other predatory fish. They are just behaving naturally and doing what nature intended for them to do and one has to remember that all or most fish are predatory to some extent.

USING PRAWNS FOR PERCH BAIT...

You sometimes hear of specimen perch being caught on prawns...

I never managed to get my large 'specimen' perch to eat prawns. I tried him on both regular prawns and 'king' prawns but he simply refused to recognise them as a food source. He preferred lobworms, sticklebacks, bullheads and other small 'micro' fish.

REARING BABY 'MICRO' PERCH

A few years after this I caught and reared half a dozen or so tiny perch. They too refused to recognise small fragments of chopped prawns as food. They too preferred worms and other live food. I introduced some 'micro' chub and the chub instantly began to feed on the chopped prawns. The small perch learnt almost immediately by observing the chub that the small fragments of prawns were in fact a good food source. Once the perch had learnt to identify the prawns as food (from the chubs example) I could remove the chub and the perch would never forget from that moment on that prawns were food! The baby perch seemed to learn things first time (at once) from mere observation alone...

THE PERCH'S PRIMITIVE DEFENSES...

The perch has a sharp, spiny, dorsal fin and spiked gills, but more than this: The perch is a rough textured, hard bodied fish with tough scales and a back like sandpaper. Where as roach, chub and gudgeon are a very soft bodied fish. The bigger a perch gets - the more defenses he has. As he grows bigger the perch becomes a much less desirable food source. For a start, he becomes the wrong shape for swallowing! When a perch reaches about two or three pounds in weight his body is very thick and his scales have a very rough, coarse, sand-paper like texture to them, making him a less desirable food source and giving him an element of protection against jack pike but make no mistake about it a bigger pike will still eat a two or even three pound perch, although it may not be his first choice. But then again, maybe a 3 pound perch is still fair game... After all, a perch's back is nowhere near as rough as the inside of a pike's mouth!

STICKLEBACK'S...

I have observed sticklebacks attacked and instantly rejected by specimen perch which have inhaled them only to spit them back out (violently) in disgust.

I have also seen 'specimen' perch nail sticklebacks with no consequences whatsoever. A friend of mine has seen exactly the same thing: A pike attacked a stickleback only to reject it in disgust a second later. We have also caught trout with sticklebacks in their stomach and pike with sticklebacks stuck in the back of their throat.

A PIKE'S LAST MEAL CAN OFTEN BE SEEN AT THE BACK OF HIS THROAT...

If the stickleback can poke his 5 spines out quick enough, he stands a fair chance of being rejected by his predator, pike, perch, trout, chub or whatever. If he is caught unawares or 'off guard' (when his spines are down) then he will definitely be eaten.

USING STICKLEBACK'S FOR BAIT...

In the past, when I have used sticklebacks for dead bait, I have found that pike, perch and chub commit to the take if you clip off the sticklebacks 5 spines. Three on their back (average) and one on each side (near the gills). If you leave the spines on - then you may lose some fish as a consequence of this. My advice: Don't take any chances - clip the spines/spikes.

The stickleback that I am talking about is of the most common variety... It is called a 3 spined stickleback but this is really a misnomer. It has in fact 5 spines - one on each side and three on the top of the back.

There are other sticklebacks with more spines or spikes but these are rarer. I have only ever caught or seen the most common 3 (5) spined stickleback. I have scooped up so many of these in one go in a hand net that the net was literally jumping with stickleback's. They really do make great bait. Especially for chub, perch, trout and jack pike. All you have to do is float-fish them down stream on a say size 6 hook, with a small float. A lot of people don't realise it, but in the right circumstances/ environment sticklebacks can grow to over two inches long and quite fat for such a small fish. The two plus inches variety make fantastic bait! If these are not available, the smaller ones will suffice and still make great bait. Predatory fish such as pike, perch, chub and trout seem to drop all wariness or reserve when these small fish are used for bait. Floatfished downstream they make devastating bait! Even outfishing lobworms!

Try it, you'll catch loads of coarse fish species with this method.

STICKLEBACK BEHAVIOUR

I have also observed stickleback behaviour in an aquarium environment. Sticklebacks although generally of no real interest to anglers (except perhaps as bait) due to their small size are still fascinating creatures...

They can grow to about 2 inches long (or over) upon reaching maturity. The male is strikingly handsome to look at in breeding season. He has a bright red chest and a bright blue (turquoise) eye colour to help him attract a female mate.

The female is a blotchy, speckled, silvery colour. Although, they are at the very bottom of the food chain, unlike bullheads (which are a more primitive/instinctive species) stickleback's are surprisingly intelligent little creatures. They can survive being attacked/snatched by both pike and perch. Very small (micro) pike learn to avoid eating sticklebacks after feeling, experiencing their spikes/spines firsthand.

The sticklebacks can grow to be surprisingly confident and very reliant upon their very efficient but primitive defences. They will flick out their spines any time a baby pike or other fish gets too close. Since I can catch micro pike and sticklebacks of very similiar sizes (the pike are actually smaller than the stickleback's.) I have raised them up together to try to mimic the environment they live in and the behaviour which they would naturally exhibit in the wild...

Here is what I have found: Small pike will on first contact initially try to eat them but usually think better of it after first hand experience of being 'pricked' with the stickleback's sharp spikes.

PURE PREDATOR...

The first time I caught a tiny 'micro' pike of about an inch/2.5 cm's long... I brought him home with a few sticklebacks for decorative purposes - to create some visual stimulation for the pike...

Imagine my surprise when, almost immediately, upon dropping the pike into my aquarium with the two or three stickleback's my pike grabbed one of the sticklebacks and attempted to eat it! Straight away within minutes. This was NOT supposed to happen! I could see the stickleback's spines were erect and I genuinely feared that my little treasure (baby pike) might die trying to swallow the stickleback. After a hairy minute or two the pike gave up and let the stickleback go (thankfully.) After that he learned to ignore the stickleback's for a while and eat worms...

'MICRO' CHUB FEEDING BEHAVIOUR

The chub seems to be a more intelligent fish than the perch and (dare I say it) the pike...

I think the chub is a more 'intelligent' and less 'instinctive' fish. Which explains why they can so easily be 'spooked' and become very wary, when alerted to an anglers presence on the bank. In my opinion, pike, perch and catfish are very 'instinctive' fish.

Small (micro) chub, unlike pike and perch will catch sticklebacks head-first and eat them down to the two side spines and then spit them out dead. So, a stickleback's prickly spine defences are useless against a small/baby chub. I wonder how many anglers or even scientists know that? The chub seems to be a more intelligent fish than the perch and (dare I say it) the pike.

When I was a kid... Me and a friend found a load of small, dead silver fish (with their heads missing) on the bottom of a small river... Could this have been the work of young 'predatory' chub? Knowing what I know now, I would say, it's possible.

TOOTHY LITTLE CRITTERS...

Here's another observation that almost nobody knows... A small 'shoal' of stickleback's lets say 8, 10, 12 or more will take it in turns to relentlessly bite a small pike's fins (from behind.)

The small 'shoal' will sneak up behind the lone pike and specifically target or (bite) his tail fin and rear power, propulsion, 'projector' fins.

The stickleback's do this to force the small pike to leave their swim or else they will relentlessly torture him until they eventually 'immobilise' the pike by eating or biting/chewing off his soft fin tissue.

The small stickleback's do in fact possess very sharp teeth and a nasty little bite. Surprisingly, If you drop in a lobworm amongst a small shoal of stickleback's they will (eventually) tear the worm to pieces and devour it with their sharp little teeth. They are a little bit like piranha's but on a much smaller (tiny) scale.

The pike in turn will eat the stickleback's as he gets bigger but to be honest I think the stickleback's are very good at seeing off the lone pike in the same way a pack of hyena's can see off a lion by taking it in turns to bite him and attack him from behind.

The stickleback's do not do this to the little tiny (micro) pike of a similiar size but once a pike grows big enough to successfully predate on the stickleback's then that is when they employ this tactic to 'disarm' the pike.

Stickleback's as well as being intelligent are a very sociable fish and also very tame. After a very short period of time sticklebacks will eat (freeze dried) bloodworms out of the palm of your hand. They are clever little fish.

The sticklebacks fin bite does seem to harrass or distress the young, juvenile pike enough to put him off hunting/feeding altogether...

CHAPTER 14. DOZENS OF TOP TIPS...

PERIODICALLY CHECK/EXAMINE ROD EYES

I know that it is not very exciting (but it is essential.) Before and after every fishing session you should periodically check the eyes of your fishing rod to assess for any 'wear and tear' (damage) that may have occurred to the plastic circle or 'eyes' of your fishing rods whilst fishing or whilst your rods are in storage or transit. I know it's boring but unknown rod 'eye' damage can cause friction/line damage (heating, weakening or 'fraying') of the line, snappages, and ultimately lost fish! Be prepared - don't take any chances! It ain't worth it!

LINE...

LINE FAULTS

Check your line for faults at the beginning and end of each fishing session. Line faults or points of weakness can be caused by friction/abrasion... I.E. tight line rubbing on rod rings or reel bale arms or caused by snags, Brambles, thorn bushes, overgrown hedges etc. If in doubt clip off at least the last 1ft of line from your reel or preferably the last 3 - 6ft or even the last nine feet - a full rod length of line.

LINE STRENGTH OR BREAKING STRAIN

For my pike fishing I like to use a good quality, time tested and reliable 12 - 15lb line that I can put a lot of faith in, and I know isn't going to let me down at the crucial moment by breaking off on a fish or snag or tangling into a 'birds nest' when I cast out.

If your line breaks off once too often or keeps tangling up into birds nests then either you've got too much line on your reel or you need to change your line for something better quality. I like Sylcast and Maxima.

Cheap, low quality line tends to tangle up on the cast or snap off unexpectedly out of the blue when under pressure. I would recommend a maximum of about 15lb (mono) and a minimum of about 12lbs (mono) due to the very high likelihood/risk of breakages due to snags, overhanging and submerged trees, logs, bushes, rocks etc.

LINE COLOUR

I don't think that line colour is all that important when it comes to lure fishing. I once caught a 15lb carp on bright orange, fluorescent 13lb line. I tend to use a gold, light brown or yellow coloured line and I never seem to have any problems catching fish. I have also used light and dark green lines with success and would have no qualms about using the clear or white lines that tend to come with new reels. I also use dark brown lines and catch fish all the time using them.

As a rule I would say dull, drab colours that blend in with their surroundings and match nature are to be favoured over bright or strong colours that stand out.

For example:
Yellow or Gold matches a sandy riverbed.
Light or dark green matches weed growth or water colouration.
Brown matches silt or rocks on the bottom of a lake or riverbed, or muddy water conditions such as rain or flood conditions.
Clear matches crystal clear water in good weather conditions.

LINE QUALITY AND STRENGTH

I think line quality, reliability, durability, abrasion resistance and strength are far more important qualities than line colour which can be superficial. That being said, if anything I would avoid bright, obvious 'luminous' lines such as sea-fishing lines tend to be.

LINE THICKNESS

I don't think that line thickness is that important either as long as you're sensible and stick to 12 - 15lb breaking strain mono or thereabouts. After all the likelihood is that your wire leader is going to be thicker than your main-line anyway.

BRAID

I don't use and would never recommend braid for lure fishing as I don't get on with it. I find it limits casting distance too much due to it holding 'water weight' and not coming off the reel as smoothly as mono when casting out.

I like to use big/oversized reel spools that hold a lot of line to maximise casting distance and what I like to call lure 'exposure.' Braid is useful if you are fishing at relatively close range and line strength is more important than casting distance. I tend to use my braid for stitching up things like holes in my army trousers! Due to it's super strong qualities.

However if you do choose to use braid for live or dead baiting for its 'strength' qualities (and ability to cut through weed.) You could realistically use anything from 20lb breaking strain on up to 50 or even 60lbs breaking strain due to braid being lower diameter than mono. Light braid (10 - 25 lb breaking strain) is fine for spinning. Heavy braid (30 - 60 lb bs) is fine for deadbaiting.

KNOTS

KNOTS STRENGTH

Please bear in mind when buying or selecting line that line can lose 10 - 30% of its strength due to knots (depending on the knot used.) Even when the knot has been expertly tied.

RECOMMENDED KNOTS...

<u>THE GRINNER KNOT</u>

My favourite knot is the 4 or preferably the 5 turn Grinner knot. It is very neat, and ultra strong and reliable. Once you have learnt how to tie it properly it only takes about ten seconds to tie! The beauty of this knot is that it does not choke or strangle the line when under pressure or tension. This is a knot that you can have 100% confidence in every time you fish. I believe in it completely and trust it implicitly. This knot has never, ever let me down. Occasionally, others have. I have to say I prefer to use five turns rather than four as it gives me that bit more confidence in my knot.

<u>THE SEVEN TURN BLOOD KNOT</u>

I used this knot for about twenty years. All in all it is a pretty safe, strong, reliable knot when tied correctly. It is pretty neat and very easy to tie. It is safe as long as you leave on a sufficient tag end to allow for line or knot slippage. However, this knot has let me down a few times as it does have a tendency to slip under pressure or when using certain types of thick, shiny, glossy lines. It also has a tendency to strangulate or choke the line when under great pressure or tension sometimes resulting in line breakage or knot failure. It is quick and easy to tie but it is my firm belief that the grinner knot is a 'superior' much more reliable, and safer knot, as it cannot slip or strangulate the line. It is not the fish you have to worry about (most of the time) it's the snags that cause you line breakages. That's why I recommend using strong lines and good (reliable) knots. They will save you a lot of time, money, and frustration in the long run.

<u>FULL BLOOD KNOT</u> (For tying line to line.)

Use less overall turns depending on the thickness of the line. As a rough guide: Use a maximum of 7 turns each way on thin, light lines and a minimum of 3 turns each way on thick, heavy lines.

<u>TIPS ON TYING KNOTS</u>

Never rush tying your knots! Always lubricate the line/knot with clean water or saliva to prevent 'lineburn' or heat friction from weakening the line/knot.

Pull the knot as S-L-O-W-L-Y as possible to avoid creating heat friction and to avoid faults and weaknesses developing in the line.

Leave a little bit of line left over at the knot say at least a few millimetres to allow for the knot slipping under pressure from heavy, hard fighting fish or tough snags.

Use nail clippers to trim knots neatly (instead of teeth) to avoid weills disease. Always leave at least a couple of millimetres or so of line as a precaution (in case your knot slips.)

Always use the grinner knot when attaching your main line to your reel spool... (That way the knot won't 'slip.')

Don't forget to set your front or rear drag (reel clutch) correctly...

If it is too loose you will lose fish on the 'strike.' If it is too tight it may not give line at the right moment and you may get snapped off by a big fish.

Always remember to 'reset' your drag after you have been snagged up... (It is very easy to forget.)

Always check the weather report and dress (appropriately) for the occasion.

<u>USING WADERS SAFELY</u>

Wear wellington boots, thigh or chest waders (be extra careful with these) to open up a river, pond or lake and be able to cast out in overgrown, awkward places where there are bushes and overhanging trees etc. Where other fishermen cannot reach or get to, and fish may never have seen a bait or lure before.

Be careful not to let the water go over the top of your waders and fill them. Especially if you are wearing chest waders. This has happened to me whilst wearing thigh waders on a number of occasions... The best thing to do is to empty the water out of your waders asap. The water can damage your mobile phone (thus potentially cutting you off and 'isolating' you in an emergency situation.) Also, you can get cold very quickly wearing wet clothes and you don't want to catch hypothermia! The simple solution is: Don't wade too deep!

If in doubt, always play it safe. Ideally, you want to be able to see the bottom from the surface and under foot should be hard like rock, stone, or gravel. I know I am stating the obvious here but never wade out in very deep water (where you cannot see the bottom.) Or in muddy or silty water where the bottom is 'sinky' like quick sand. It ain't worth it! As always safety is paramount. You've got to use your loaf.

STAY SAFETY CONSCIOUS

Always be safety conscious... Wear a floatation device or 'life jacket' when fishing deep or dangerous water. As a rule I will only wade out on solid ground/rock or hard, compact sand or gravel and preferably where I can see the bottom. I never wade out in 'sinky' silt or mud. I did that once before, years ago and ended up, up to my chest in water. Be smart, it's not worth it!

AVOIDING SLIPS, TRIPS AND FALLS...

As you get older your balance is not as good as it once was and it becomes more important to avoid slips, trips and falls...

The best advice that I can give you is to choose your footwear very carefully and always avoid wearing trainers...

You have far less chance of slipping when you are wearing waterproof leather boots or wellington boots as they have much better 'tread' or grip on the soles of the feet.

Watch out for silty, slippy, muddy banks and marshy, unstable riverbanks that collapse or give way beneath your feet...

There are various other 'hazards' and dangers: As my old mum used to say "You've got to keep your wits about you!"

BEWARE OF ELECTRICITY PYLONS!

Always be on the lookout for electricity pylons. Never fish near them as you cannot accurately judge the casting distance of projectiles in mid-air (at height) properly. I once accidently cast a spinner over a line between two posts... Luckily for me it was only a telephone line!

Never fish on in a thunder storm, it is not worth it! Take your rods down and seek shelter under a bridge or something similiar - not under a big tree! Go home, or wait until you are sure that the storm has passed before you carry on fishing!

Be on the lookout for electricity pylons - don't fish near them as you cannot judge casting distance at height in the air properly or accurately. I once accidently cast a spinner over a line between two posts... Luckily for me it was a telephone line!

THUNDERSTORMS

Never fish on in a thunder storm - it's not worth it! Take you're rods down and seek shelter under a bridge or something similiar - not under a big tree! Go home or wait until you are sure that the storm has passed before you carry on fishing!

FIRST AID

Always carry a small first aid kit, antibacterial handcream and waterproof plasters with you at all times when you are out fishing.

LEPTOSPIROSIS OR 'WEILLS' DISEASE

Be aware of the risks of Leptospirosis or weills disease... read up on Leptospirosis or Weills disease which is found in rats and sometimes dogs urine. Rats are incontinent (pee everywhere all the time.) When their urine finds it's way into rivers, streams, ponds and lakes then the germ or bacteria is spread in the water. It is most common in stagnant lakes and ponds but can be found rivers, streams or anywhere. Leptospirosis can get into your body through a cut or graze - such as a treble hook in the finger or a cut from a pike's teeth whilst unhooking a lively pike. Through water splashing into your eyes - such as off your line when you are reeling in or pulling weed off your line. Through your mouth via food or drink contamination such as washing fish slime off your hands in the water and then eating crisps or a sandwich. Or through putting a can of drink in the water to keep it cool and then getting a small trace of infected water in your mouth. Weills disease can kill. The symptoms are flu like symptoms three days to three weeks after infection occurs.

If you suspect that you have come into contact with weills disease whilst out fishing then go and see your doctor immediately as it is curable if caught in good time.

Always practise good hygiene whilst out fishing and remember that your hands probably aren't clean so be careful when eating and drinking. Always carry a good antibacterial hand gel as a bare minimum precaution...

Try to carry a small first aid kit, antibacterial handcream and waterproof plasters with you at all times when you are out fishing.

PEG MAINTENANCE

If necessary, carry a small gardening saw, or some handy loppers to cut or prune back any fishing pegs overgrown with trees, branches, or bushes. This will enable you to cast out better with more ease or even cut, or saw out a brand new "secret" peg in a previously wild, overgrown, and unfished location as long as you have permission to do so and won't get yourself into trouble. This is when and where you really do get lucky and strike gold.

Don't get sunburned! Use overhead trees or bushes for shade, stay covered up or use sun cream. Keep your arms etc covered up or use mosquito or insect repellant to keep the horse flies and midges at bay.

Always carry nail clippers for cutting line and a pair of extra long nosed plyers for unhooking any (unexpected) h-u-g-e pike! Sometimes scissors, and wire cutters can come in handy too...

CHAPTER 15. FINAL THOUGHTS...

In all endeavours it is very easy to become complacent and stay within your comfort zone. People tend to stick with the familiar. What worked yesterday will work today. Unfortunately that is not always so. It's that old maxim "if it's not broke then don't fix it." Unfortunately, sometimes it is broke and it needs fixing. Only, we don't know it. Sometimes fishermen "stick with what they know" for years. Unfortunately what worked in yesteryear may not work today, especially when it comes to fishing and lures. Fish do indeed become 'wise.' In my experience it is very easy for an experienced fisherman to stagnate. If you are not experimenting and learning new things all the time, then you are not developing or growing as a fisherman. I, like all fishermen, fell into this pattern of behaviour and my catch rates went down and I just could not understand why? Then I started experimenting again... Trying new techniques, new methods, new baits, new lures, fishing new waters, broadening my horizons and seeking pastures new... Reading up on fish and fishing... And guess what? I began to grow again and evolve into the successful fisherman that I have become today.

STUCK IN A RUT

I have old friends that I used to fish with almost 20 years ago. I see them and guess what they are doing? Exactly the same thing that they were doing 20 years ago! They are fishing the same old places, with the same old methods and getting the same old results. Well actually, they're not getting the same old results (the fish are getting wiser) they catch less and less fish until they eventually just get used to blanking and accept it as the norm! They are just happy to get out of the door and get away from the missus and kids! If they catch one fish in a day then they think that's a result! Talk about stuck in a rut! Fish do indeed get wise, especially in response to fishing 'pressure.'

SIZE MATTERS...

You will have noticed throughout this book that I am not one for overly 'fixating on' or bragging about weights and measurements. There are enough fishing books (and exaggerated magazine accounts) that go on and on about weights and measurements... It's all 20 pounds this and 30 pounds that... Each to their own. The aim of my book is to inspire people to go out fishing whatever level they are at...

They say that: "Comparison is the thief of joy!"

If you are a discerning reader then you may have noticed that I am sometimes reluctant to disclose the locations of some of my captures to others in my immediate vicinity (geographically speaking.) It's not that I don't want others to catch them - it's just that I might like to catch them again one day! When you've seen a 25 pound pike needlessly lying dead on the bank, it makes you think...

I'm not talking about further afield in the wider angling community/world but just locally to me geographically speaking. I would rather 'team up' with a good pike fisherman and then if someone else catches the fish that I am after at least I am there to see it! I'm happy to be the man behind the lens. I can really appreciate a big pike that way. Some fishermen just don't appreciate pike. They 'cull' a specimen pike and think that they've done the world a favour! Some fishermen regard pike as the absolute scum of the earth... I have even heard pike referred to as 'vermin.'

SCARFACE

I once saw a 'specimen' pike of about 20 pounds or so in weight in a clear, shallow stretch of river... One side of it's face was badly damaged and torn to bits! It looked like somebody had put a 'banger' (firework) in its mouth and let it go off! "Night line" I said to myself. I can only deduce that it was caught on a night line and managed to fight itself free during the course of the night - badly tearing up one side of it's face in the process. To be honest: Judging by it's appearance - that pike was lucky to even survive the encounter.

BEAUTY AND MAJESTY

I on the other hand, have an exceedingly great appreciation for the beauty and majesty of all pike... From the tiniest, newborn 'micro' pike with their cute little snouts! I simply cannot 'resist' keeping them in an aquarium every chance I get! I will never get tired of looking at those little beauties and watching them grow up! (Monsters in miniature.) They always put a big smile on my face! To the big toothy critters... Those huge 'prehistoric' monsters that only a few fishermen are ever lucky enough to see in the wild (never mind catch.) I simply love them all!

ON THE OUTSIDE LOOKING IN...

The size of the fish you catch is not always an accurate indicator of your experience or 'true' ability as a fisherman. Sometimes it is more of an indicator of the quality of the fish/fishing that is immediately available to you, right on your doorstep...

Unfortunately, for most of us it is not a level playing field and life is not always fair. Some people are lucky or fortunate enough to have great fishing available to them (all year round) right on their doorstep! If you live on or near the Norfolk Broads you might be one of them! Whilst others (the rest of us) might have to drive or travel miles out of our way for a decent days fishing! Without the benefit of having any local knowledge. It can be frustrating at times...

I remember once enquiring about fishing a beautiful coarse fishing lake I spotted out in the countryside... Only to be told that the fee for joining said 'syndicate' was £2000! (this was over 20 years ago now.) And that membership was by "invitation only." I knew the owner's son. I worked with him for nearly 4 years, but I still couldn't get an invite! It turned out that there were only about 15 'members' in total. All old men, and close, personal friends of the owner! From the outside it looked like fort knox! On the inside - the garden of Eden! Sadly, I was only ever "on the outside looking in."

THE 'BEST' PIKE FISHERMEN...

Live baiting is undoubtably the most devastating, irresistable method of catching big pike...

The best pike fishermen understand that 'livebaits' make the best baits (the very best baits.) Ultimately, live baits will often 'outfish' deadbaits and lures. You can catch lots of pike on lures. You can catch big pike on lures and (more often) deadbaits (big pike turn scavenger as they get bigger and older.)

Big pike do indeed get wise with time and age especially when under heavy fishing 'pressure.' Pike CAN get wise to lures. They can, I have seen/experienced this personally on some 'hard' waters.

The crux of it is this: Big pike do not and cannot get 'wise' to live fish. They have to rely and depend upon live fish. They have to hunt and feed upon live fish. They are always going to be the most susceptible to being caught on live fish or live bait. Always.

GOING 'LIVE'

So in effect, the best pike fisherman is the one who understands this and has the most readily available, reliable source of 'good quality' live baits to hand! That is why certain men (well known for catching big pike) have in the past invested in 'fully oxygenated' live bait tanks/industrial plastic containers etc for this very purpose and some of them have even admitted to having containers for live bait storage built into their motorised boats! I am not one of these men. I don't own a boat (unfortunately.) My 'pets' are just that - pets. I keep them for a year at most (until they get too big for my tanks) and then I release them back into the wild where I caught them and continue the same process again and again, year after year.

Depending where you fish or what country you live in - live baiting may be legal and common place/acceptable or illegal, unacceptable or at the very least frowned upon. I'm not a massive advocate of 'live baiting' but technically even a worm or maggot is a 'live' bait! I am just telling it the way it is...

A specimen pike is unlikely to get wise to 'live' fish. I am more inclined and feel more comfortable with using lures, deadbaits and 'micro' baits such as bullheads, gudgeon, stickleback's and minnows for my predator fishing - the type of fish that anglers generally do not bother to fish for/aren't interested in catching due to their small size. The smaller the bait is - the more comfortable I am with using it and the less it bothers my conscience.

THE 'BIG PIKE MEN'

As a man 'in the know' I'm just letting you know that some of the really 'big pike men' are live bait men. They primarily rely/depend on live baits to get results. Not all of them. Some of them are deadbait men (like me) and some of them prefer to troll big lures from the back of their boats... (If only.)

It took me along time to realize it but 'big' pike prefer big lures in the same way that 'big' pike prefer big fish or big 'baits.' It took me years to realize this but that's just the way it is... I still prefer to start off with smaller lures (such as the 4 inch minnow shaped ones) just in case there are any smaller mouthed predator's such as perch, trout or chub in the immediate vicinity. Then I will stick on a big lure for the pike and catfish (just in case...)

IT'S ALL RELATIVE....

Nowadays, I am all about fishing for pure pleasure, relaxation and enjoyment. I want to inspire people to go out fishing. I have an uncle. He is in his 70's now. His 'personal best' record pike is 38 lb's. Suffice to say that I am jealous and envious of him!!

At the end of the day: Size is all relative: When I was a young lad a four pound pike was a 'monster' to me and my young friends. Come to think of it a one pound trout seemed 'pretty big' too back in those early days...

To give you some perspective: I once saw an 'antique' (stuffed) pike in a glass case on a wall. It weighed fifteen pounds - only fifteen pounds! But somebody (back in the day) was so delighted with their capture of a 15 pounds pike that they decided to have it stuffed! Nowadays, a 15 pound pike is not even regarded as a 'specimen' pike. You have to catch a twenty pounder for it to be regarded as a true specimen! But, nonetheless a fifteen pounds pike is still a big fish, and I for one will never stop enjoying catching 15 pounds pike, or ten pounds pike for that matter! A 15 pounder will get your photo in the fishing magazines but it wont get you in the Guinness book of records!

IT'S NOT ALL ABOUT 'PERSONAL BESTS'

I remember a few years ago... I was fishing with a 16 year old lad who had just recently discovered the joys of fishing for pike on lures! He had only been fishing for about a couple of years... I hooked and landed a nice pike after leisurely playing it in with one hand. Throughout the tussle he kept badgering me about "being careful and not losing the fish!" After landing the fish, he turned to me and said: "If I had caught that fish it would have been my personal best!" "But this is not my first rodeo" I replied. "I have done this many times." If you have never caught a ten pound fish then a ten pound fish is a big fish to you. I remember catching my first proper pike as a young boy... (It only weighed four pounds!) But it seemed huge to me and my friends back then - a real life 'monster.'

Ultimately, fish 'size' is all relative to fishing experience. We are all at different stages of our fishing 'journey' but at the end of the day, you have to enjoy the journey, it's the journey that counts.

YOU HAVE GOT TO ENJOY YOUR FISHING...

Like most things in life, fishing can become extremely competitive (if you let it.) The problem with this is that it becomes all about 'specimen hunting,' records, and personal bests. I have moved beyond that, I prefer to fish for pure pleasure and enjoyment...

I can remember fishing the Norfolk Broads on a boat back in 1998... I was only eighteen years old at the time. It is memorable to me for several reasons... Here are a couple of them:

1. I caught my first ever eel... I have never caught one locally ever since! (They are an endangered species.)

2. I caught my first ever ruffe...

The ruffe we were catching were only a few inches long (they don't grow very big) and probably only weighed a few ounces, but I had never seen one before. They are a beautiful little fish and we don't get them where I live... It was refreshing to catch and see two new species of fish that I had never seen/caught before.

I remember one time I was fishing a small waterfall/river for brown and common trout on large freelined lobworms and I caught a greedy, gutsy, little bullhead!

Another time I was spinning a midlands canal (hoping to catch a double figure or 20 pound's pike.) I caught a baby jack pike that was smaller than the lure I was using! The pike was slightly longer than the lure but the circumference of the lure was bigger than the circumference of the pike!

Another time, someone I was lake fishing with 'caught' a lamprey on his lure!! Now nobody wants to catch a lamprey on a lure, but the fact is that the chances of doing this is like a billion to one! You have got to see it for what it is...

Life doesn't always go the way that you plan it and fishing is no exception to this rule. You just have to enjoy everything for what it is and take the rough with the smooth. We all like to put our best foot forward and fishermen are no different. In fact, some fishermen would have you believe that they are so accomplished that they have never made a mistake! This is codswallop, we all make mistakes - unfortunately this is how we learn (from our mistakes.) There is an old saying: "A man who has never made a mistake has never made anything."

THE 'BEST BITS'

Have you ever noticed that you never see any outtakes, deleted scenes, or a 'blooper' highlight reel at the end of a fishing program? There is a good reason for that... If you got to see all of the 'snagged' and lost lures, broken lines, lost fish, presenters and camera-men falling in the water, and general 'tomfoolery.' The 'fishermen' (presenters) wouldn't look very accomplished! The 'outakes' (reality tv) might be (longer) and more interesting than the actual program. It might look like a comedy show more than a serious fishing program. You might never tune in again! Then again, it might be hilarious! It would cheer all us 'ordinary' anglers up no end... They could call it: Laurel and Hardy go fishing... It would be like watching the 'chuckle brothers' on a fishing expedition..."To me, to you..."

THE ONE THAT GOT AWAY...

I have a confession to make... The big pike I hooked on the twelve inch, 'luminous' orange and yellow bulldawg (mentioned briefly in an earlier chapter & right at the beginning of the book) I lost it! Yep, I lost THAT fish. I know, I know. I had her inches or at the very least 'feet' away from the mouth of my 'enormous' large mouth triangular 'oversized' landing net but I just couldn't quite close the deal and convince her to get in it!

In my defense (I don't have much of one) I had never fished that stretch of river before and had no idea there were pike in there that big (or at least one rogue pike that big.) I had caught nothing all day long and that pike caught me so completely off guard with her sheer size, and tremendous, breath taking speed and aggression that in the heat of the moment - I just about shit my pants and forgot everything I ever knew about fishing! She was a super fit, massively powerful fish, due to her living at the base of a rapid waterfall/weirpool in such a fast flowing, powerful river. I have caught pike on deadbait of a 'roughly' similiar size that were at maximum weight and full of eggs but they fought nowhere and I do mean NOWHERE near as hard! This was one 'super-fit' sporting fish. I struck hard and immediately put pressure on her but I was fighting against a large, fresh, strong, fish as well as a heavy current! I struggled hard to pull her upstream and in towards the net! She fought like a wild tiger and in the midst of an exciting tail whipping, 'head thrashing' battle she managed to open her massive jaws at the last minute, and use the weight of my bulldawg to leverage and propel my 12 inch lure hopelessly up into the air with one final, devastating shake of her huge, monstrous head. I watched on helplessly as the big lure splashed back into the water. My hopes completely dashed...

In one painfully brief moment, I had just lost quite possibly the single biggest pike that I had ever hooked on a lure! I could have cried. You could argue that it was my fault for removing the large treble hook off of the bottom of the lure. If only I had left on that extra treble... To be honest: If I had left it on I would have most likely never hooked that 'crocodile' in the first place. More likely I would have been snagged up on a ton of weed! I think that pike was easily over three feet long and quite possibly twenty or more pounds in weight, but sadly we may never know! I went back to the exact same spot on one or two occasions afterwards but there was simply no sign of that fish. Hours of fishing deadbaits and even a large 'smelly' mackerel simply produced nothing. Who knows? One day, I may travel back to that big river and give it another shot... One thing's for sure, my fishing buddy is well up for it! He like me - simply could not believe his eyes that day!

HITTING ROCK BOTTOM

Another time, me and another old friend were fishing a very deep, 'wild' stretch of river. My friend (an experienced pike fisherman of many years) and may I say - an abnormally jammy lure fisherman, was using a tiny (6 gram?) spinner. His rod was bending and as he pulled on it he casually informed me that he was 'snagged' on the bottom of the river... "Impossible" I said, "the water is far too deep for that." Realizing what I was saying he began reeling in quickly and heaving on his rod. Slowly but surely this huge pike passively rose up to the top of the water column right in front of us. For a brief couple of seconds she lay motionless at the top of the water while we both looked on in shock and disbelief! This pike had bent his rod double (my friend thought that he had hooked a big log on the bottom) and here is the absolute kicker: She didn't even seem to know that she was hooked and hadn't even begun to fight back yet! But that was all about to change... Upon seeing us she went berserk! All of a sudden she kicked into gear with one almighty swipe of her huge red tail. Furiously smashing the calm surface of the water right in front of us. Immediately, my friend had all on...

Sadly, the top and bottom of it is that he lost the fish. We watched on helplessly as she swam back down to the depths, never to be seen again. In one cruel instant, my friend who was in his 30's at the time and has lure fished since he was 16 years old and worked in a fishing tackle shop (for several years.) After serving a 20 year fishing 'apprenticeship' had fallen asleep on the job and in the process lost his personal best pike. It seemed that she may have been only 'lightly' hooked after all!

THE MORAL OF THE STORY IS: THAT YOU MUST NEVER LET YOUR GUARD DOWN WHEN YOU ARE FISHING!!!!!

(Especially when you are lure fishing.)

Unfortunately, it is easier said than done... I've done it. You've done it. We've all done it!!!

It happens because: We are not the only ones hunting... (So are the pike - if you catch my drift) and we are only part timers - they are 'time served' full time, 24 hours a day hunter's... For us it's a part time hobby, for them it's a full time job - survival of the fittest. That's why they catch us off guard. They are better hunters than we are. Their senses and reflexes are much sharper and keener...

DEADWEIGHT

Okay, just one more fisherman's tale... A few years ago, I was fishing 'deep' using a good old fashioned pike spoon. I felt a heavy load on the end of my rod. I pulled hard but nothing happened! I was sure that I was snagged up on the bottom... I heaved really hard. All of a sudden my lure came loose and fluttered back up to the surface, I reeled in my line and swung the spoon into my hand. Upon examining my lure I found one single, abnormally large pike scale on the end of my treble hook!!! It seemed that I had foul hooked a huge pike, but the fish never even pulled back! "How strange" I thought to myself... To this day, the question remains: If I foul hooked a pike that day... Was it alive - or dead? Is that why it never reacted to me foul hooking it? Maybe I hooked some big, old, dead pike laying on the bottom? I guess I'll never know.

NONE OF US ARE INFALLIBLE...

If I have 'stumbled' somewhere along the way... You have to bear in mind that I have been fishing for over 30 years... Sadly, these things happen to the best of us. I have cast out lures more times than Tiger Woods has swung his golf club! (Innumerable times.) I can hit a hairs breadth (with a lure) at a hundred yards and have effortlessly put my lures in the most (snaggy) difficult to get to places on many, many occasions. I have also lost good lures in trees and bushes, and forgot to unclip my bale-arm (the ultimate school-boy error) whilst casting out a few too many times to mention! At my best, I am a super skilled lure fisherman, at my worst - a klutz/clumsy fool. Fishermen are renowned for taking pictures of the fish they catch... But what about all the ones that got away? I for one, have dropped some absolute clangers!! And if you are completely honest... The chances are, so have you! No matter, let's move on.

I have shared with you some of the best and most important tips that I have learnt over many years... I sincerely hope that they improve your fishing experience and your catch rates! And maybe, just maybe, you'll catch that fish of a lifetime - the one that always seems to get away...

THE MYSTERY OF FISHING

What is it he holds like a spear in his hands?
Each step like a whisper, soft in the sands
And what is it of the line that we feed through each eye?
The silk of the spider that catches the fly.
What is this creation on the end of his line?
That flutters like a dancer so delicate and fine,
And what is it of a lure that so captivates the mind?
Gives sight to the sightless and renders the other blind.
What is it of the rod that we hold in our hands?
A mere branch of a tree, that grows on the land,
And what is it of the flies we tie with our feathers?
That lead us out on the water in all kinds of weathers...
And what is it of a float that we watch it for hours?
It possesses no mystery nor magical powers,

And what is it of the knot that all rests upon?
The artwork and tapestry that renders weakness strong,
And what is it of the hook in which we place such faith?
To hold onto priceless treasures and deliver them back safe,
And what is it of the net that we clip to our back?
A mere stick and some string - weaved into a sack!
And what is it of the water that rushes quickly by?
Nothing but the raindrops that fall from the sky?
And what is it of the river that dampens our feet?
The fishermans lifeblood, his very heartbeat.

AFTERWORD

Thank you for reading this book.

I hope that you have been amused, entertained, and inspired...

If you enjoyed my book, please don't forget to leave a positive rating/short review online (much appreciated.)

Now, what are you waiting for? Get out there and catch some fish!!

The Author

Made in United States
North Haven, CT
04 November 2024

59873448R00143